MIRANDA'S
DAILY DOSE
OF SUCH FUN

Also by Miranda Hart

Is It Just Me?
The Best of Miranda
Peggy and Me

MIRANDA'S DAILY DOSE OF SUCH FUN

MIRANDA HART

• •

HODDER

First published in Great Britain in 2017 by
Hodder & Stoughton
An Hachette UK company

1

First published in paperback in 2017

A CIP catalogue record for this title is available from the British Library

ISBN 978 1 473 65645 1

Typeset in Wunderlich by Hewer Text UK Ltd, Edinburgh
Printed and bound by Clays Ltd, St Ives plc

Hodder & Stoughton policy is to use papers that are natural, renewable
and recyclable products and made from wood grown in sustainable
forests. The logging and manufacturing processes are expected to
conform to the environmental regulations of the country of origin.

Hodder & Stoughton Ltd
Carmelite House
50 Victoria Embankment
London EC4Y 0DZ
www.hodder.co.uk

In memory of one my best friends Joanna Dugdale, aka Bella
23rd September 1973 – 23rd May 2016

She always had the capacity for seeing the fun,
the silly and the positive.
And she gave me two of the ideas for this book.

INTRODUCTION

Well hello to you and welcome to *Miranda's Daily Dose of Such Fun*. What is it, Miranda? Well, thank you for asking. Put simply, it's a book that gives you a joy- filled task for every day of the year in order to help make your life more engaging, caring and fun. These are small gestures but with the potential to make a big difference to you and those around you. Or, if you want the more highbrow version of what I mean, here's a quote by C.S. Lewis that has always inspired me:

'The smallest good act today is the strategic point from which, months later, you may be able to go on to victories you never dreamed of.'

This book came into being as a result of my own experiences with anxiety. Over the years, due to an anxiety disorder, I have had sensations that have ranged from a general underlying sense of danger and fear; to being physically hampered by various injuries and illnesses making it hard or impossible to do what I wanted to do; to being completely immobilized and housebound.

I have had a very blessed life and I count myself incredibly lucky. But in my own relative way it hasn't all been easy. Life during times of acute anxiety has been like wading through treacle and on bad days even getting to the end of the street to post a letter was hard, such was the extreme level of fear in my body. All things that are very hard to explain, as you'll know if you've ever experienced anything similar.

When I was particularly unwell with anxiety the idea for *Miranda's Daily Dose of Such Fun* came to me. I wanted to think outside of myself, and do something for others who might also be suffering from anxiety or depression. And also for those who may not have disorders as such, but find they are often stressed, too busy, given to excessive worrying and naturally inclined to feeling negative about themselves and life. That is, for most of us!

What I have found is that once you make the choice to challenge the bad habits of stress and anxiety; to remind your body that you are strong and the thoughts are just thoughts, and the feelings are just feelings, moving in to wellness and an anxiety free life can be surprisingly simple.

My *Daily Dose of Such Fun* offers some fun and simple daily tasks to help you move away from stress and anxiety. Every day do something jolly that you can look back on with a smile and be grateful for knowing it has brought kindness to others at the same time. Doing something positive regularly and repetitively can gradually help to replace old anxious and negative patterns with new happier and more hopeful ones. All my ideas, however silly they may seem, are a genuine and healthy way to change how you feel. And if you think some of them are too silly or too childish then try to free yourself up, go for it, knowing the more diverted you are from your negative thoughts the better.

I spent too many years trying to cover up my anxiety, boredom or sadness with food and television, for example. Although both those things are wonderful and serve a great purpose, habitually using them to 'numb out' doesn't work and can just perpetuate the problem. (Others may use alcohol, relationships, gambling, or spending, for example, as ways to numb out.) A *Daily Dose of Such Fun* will help towards changing your state of mind. And don't worry, many of the tasks include food and television!

If you feel yourself resisting change then I will say this: you are a uniquely brilliant human being on this planet for a reason. You have been given life at this time because the world needs a *you* in it. We need you to fulfill your purpose, to be free to be who you want to be, and to not let anything stop you from having a full life. You are loved, you are unique, you are beautiful. You know you don't want to stay angry, or hurt, or stressed, or tired, or anxious, or depressed. You know deep down you have a life you want to live. And I want to encourage you to realize that moving away from your fears *is* possible and *is* worth it.

I have made the ideas in this book as universal (and either free or cheap) as possible, but of course sometimes you may need to adapt the tasks to make them work for you. And if there are songs or talks or people that I refer to that you don't know, then get thee to YouTube, they will all be on there.

So here's to your daily doses of such fun. I wrote them for you. It helped me enormously to write them. And I really hope they help you move towards a calmer and happier life, and that you have SUCH FUN doing them.

Love Miranda x

P.S. Please reach out to friends, family and your doctor if you are needing support or think you might be suffering from depression. There is no shame in any feelings of vulnerability however they may manifest.

P.P.S. Please remember these daily activities are suggestions for FUN. They are to be done with a light touch and kindness to others. I will not BE responsible for teasing and meanness and certainly do not want to hear about any bust ups, crashes, total wildness or public disturbances thank you very much! Go gently.

P.P.P.S. All the royalties from the sale of this book in the UK will be donated to Miranda's Fund, supporting young people to improve their emotional well-being, including those experiencing anxiety and depression. Miranda's Fund is managed by Comic Relief. If you feel you can donate further then you can do so by going to: www.comicrelief.com/mirandasfund

JANUARY

• •

JANUARY 1ST

The beginning of a new year – a time for hope and change. Don't be overwhelmed; change is possible. What you want to achieve *is* possible. So let's start the New Year with our first Dollop O' Such Fun.

Stand on a chair in front of your loved ones and say, 'Whether I keep any New Year resolutions or not, I am an amazing, beautiful, unique human being. Please applaud me.'

NOTE: As it's New Year's Day I also suggest putting on a suitable anthem song and instigate a dance and/or sing-a-long. How about *Don't stop Believing*?

JANUARY 2ND

Winter nights don't need to feel long or lonely.

Invite a friend over (or this is equally fun on your own). Get some popcorn and watch a film or some TV of your choice (I hear Miranda *is excellent). Make sure it's popcorn you have to make yourself. When it starts coming to life in the saucepan, invent a "pop dance" as they pop. Music optional. Ideally it would be some kind of . . . POP! Perhaps open a bottle and enjoy the POP of that, too.*

Happy POP-tastic day.

● ●

JANUARY 3RD

If your New Year resolution was a diet and you've broken it already, then break it in style and don't feel guilty about it. Either start again tomorrow or take the pressure off a strict diet and just try and eat a fraction less each day and walk about a bit more; you'll lose the weight.

Have a banquet. Have three courses of your favourite foods. Lay the table like they would in Downton Abbey. *Ask a friend to be a waiter! Candles. Tuck napkins into your chest as if you were Henry VIII. Dine in style. Savour the tastes. Diet or no diet, it's good to have a FEAST DAY.*

JANUARY 4TH

We all have an inner child that needs to express its joy and freedom. It's so easy to ignore our playful needs as an adult by getting bogged down in the strains of achieving and doing.

Get your friends or family to dance or do silly moves across every zebra crossing (ideally make up a short routine for it). Don't waste the cars' time too much, but cross in a way that will make the people waiting laugh. SUCH FUN.

● ●

JANUARY 5TH

I believe adults need to reclaim the gallop from toddlers – it's not fair that it's not socially acceptable for us to gallop. Why should they have the monopoly on galloping? Especially when it brings a surprising amount of joy. So today have your seasonal WINTER GALLOP!

Gallop in a public place – train station, office, your street, supermarket. A spontaneous gallop. Making horse noises or using an imaginary whip are optional.

JANUARY 6TH

One of the key points of these Such Fun daily ideas is to help us all get back in touch with the nature of playing. To have moments in the day when we are connecting with others – in love, laughing, playing, or just being. There is a brilliant TED Talk that says it all.

Watch the TED Talk by Shonda Rhimes called 'My year of saying yes to everything'. It's AMAZING.

● ●

JANUARY 7TH

Life can be very simply, but uniquely, more playful.

The key with finding more joy in life is finding it in the simplest of things. We don't need to strive for success or money or possessions to find joy. Joy can be found anywhere despite our circumstances.

Give a lollipop to a lollipop lady. Brilliant. Make her day and yours.

JANUARY 8TH

Are you someone who finds that long winter nights get you down? Personally I see them as an excuse for nice early bedtimes. But if bed time is getting boring for you and your partner . . . well, romance needn't be dead or serious.

When you take your clothes off tonight, do a silly striptease for your loved one, ideally to The Stripper *music. Surprise the heck out of them. Throw those clothes into the laundry basket as sexily as you dare!*

NOTE: This can EASILY be done just for your own amusement if you live alone. Trust me, I've done it! (There's an image . . .)

● ●

JANUARY 9TH

Don't know about you but sometimes life feels all a bit much. I just want to hide and ideally not even get out of bed, especially in the winter. Well, let's turn that depressed feeling into something fun.

Choose a friend or family member. Wrap each other in as big a duvet as possible. Use tape or string to hold the duvets up, then SUMO! Or just fall to the floor and bash into walls. SUCH FUN!

JANUARY 10TH

Anyone else dream of being a pop or rock star? It's important to have dreams, but sadly some of the crazier ones don't always come true. However, there's nothing to say you can't find your way to fulfil them in your own unique way.

Turn the lights off in the kitchen. Put on a favourite song. Open the fridge. Imagine the light is a spotlight on a massive stage. Grab a wooden spoon for a microphone and PERFORM . . .

● ●

JANUARY 11TH

Community and fellowship are key to good health and well-being. But we are often all too isolated. Even when we are together, we can be in our own worlds.

I dare you to start a sing-a-long on your commuter train or bus today. Start singing and ask if people want to join in. It might be easier with a few friends. It would be AMAZING if the whole carriage and bus could go to work that day with a hearty sing-a-long. How about Always Look on the Bright Side of Life. *Or the Muppet song. Or have a sing-a-long on the way to work in your car – wind down the windows and try to get people to join in when you hit traffic.*

NOTE: PLEASE let me know if anyone achieved this (ideally with footage), it would make me SO happy!

JANUARY 12TH

Who says there is no such thing as a free lunch in this life?
NOT ME!

*Today, spread the love . . . If you can, buy the person in front of
you or behind you in the queue their lunch (at the supermarket,
at Pret, at Starbucks or the canteen). SO NICE OF YOU. Tell
them, 'There IS such a thing as a free lunch. Now, go and have
a lovely afternoon.' They'll feel great, you'll feel great, what's
not to love?*

● ●

JANUARY 13TH

How is January going so far? Do you feel like you've got into a
boring routine already? Are those negative habits creeping
back in despite an energised start to the year? Well, don't
worry, today you can break the negativity and have a simple,
fun moment by spicing up your life.

Put on Spice up your Life *by the Spice Girls and sort out your
SPICES! Throw away the out of date ones, put them in alpha-
betical order and use one you haven't used for a while in your
dinner. Literally, SPICE UP YOUR LIFE!*

JANUARY 14TH

Singing is great for the soul and body. It gets the lungs going, helps you breathe more slowly, it opens up the throat, and can have a very soothing effect on the nervous system. Which is why I will always be the first to suggest a sing-a-along.

Put on a song of your choice and sing horribly out of tune for the whole of it. FUN. This can be extra fun with a friend. Harmonize in awful ways! If you happen to be tone deaf – try and sing IN tune!

• •

JANUARY 15TH

Yesterday we sang the January blues away. Today, we dance. Dancing lightens the soul. A tense body is more likely to lead to anxious thoughts. Changing the state of your body changes the state of your mind so get your body moving freely and differently.

Put on a song of your choice and dance COMPLETELY OUT OF TIME! Hilarious.

NOTE: If you do this with the family, then perhaps do some Dad dancing. Get some embarrassing moves from your Dad or Mum.

JANUARY 16TH

Show your loved ones what you mean to them. Receiving love and feeling important to someone is vital to everyone's emotional health. We all need to feel known and understood.

When you get back from work, or school, create a massive reunion. Run towards your loved one as if you are in the closing moments of a romantic film. Give them an enormous hug. Sing the classic, 'I love you baby, and if it's quite all right I need you baby to warm the lonely nights. I love you baby, trust in me when I say . . .' right in their ear!

● ●

JANUARY 17TH

I often bung on a Christmas film in January to remind me of the Christmas spirit.

If you haven't seen it before – watch It's a Wonderful Life. *Or watch it again. It will make you realize life can be . . . WONDERFUL. You just need to see it the right way.*

NOTE: You could also play the song *It's a Wonderful Life* today. And remember by doing these Daily Doses of Fun you are making new memories and life *is* getting more wonderful.

JANUARY 18TH

I believe in eating "little and often". Although I get into trouble by making it 'a lot and as often as possible'! Food can easily become a friend when we are anxious. It's important to recognize if we are doing too much comfort eating and find healthier ways to soothe ourselves. I have to exercise a lot of self-control around food. But I allow myself treats (very important) and one thing I love is a fry-up. But there's never time in the morning, is there? Fear not, I am with solution.

Have a fry-up for DINNER in the evening. BRILLIANT.

Who says fry-ups are only for breakfast? NOT ME!

● ●

JANUARY 19TH

If you've found yourself joining a gym in classic New Year resolution style and you already can't bear to go (don't blame you, I hate gyms – THEY SMELL OF CROTCH – go for nice walks outside instead for exercise) then, well, this is a bit cheeky but I dare you . . .

Get some snacks. Place them evenly apart along the treadmill. Start the treadmill and quickly go and lie down at the end of it. Catch as many snacks as you can in your mouth! Encourage fellow gym buddies to play.

JANUARY 20TH

Did you know that orchestra conductors are the least likely type of professionals to have heart attacks? Moving the arms gets blood flowing to the arteries better than any other exercise.

Put on some classical music or the fabulous Classic FM and pretend to be a conductor. Use drumsticks, wooden spoons or even sticks as batons. Conduct as if your life depends on it!

NOTE: If you are with friends you could ask them to play certain imaginary instruments and be the leader of an imaginary orchestra. WHAT LARKS!

• •

JANUARY 21ST

Some days we just feel down, like a black cloud is following us around and we have no idea why. But there's always something to be grateful for, and turning our minds to gratitude is a sure fire way to feel happier.

Say to yourself: 'I am alive in this very day. I don't know what is going to happen tomorrow, so let's just make the best of today.' Try and appreciate five things during the day, however small.

I'll start: Today I am grateful for cups of tea, warm socks, my dog, my bed, and cold crisp air.

JANUARY 22ND

Just to remind you, this book-ette is all about breaking the patterns of the negative. Bringing moments to sparkle up life, to create new memories and push out the old anxious habits. I'm trying not to be too cheeky with some Such Fun suggestions, but I can't resist this one.

Put random items into a friend's (or stranger's) supermarket trolley when they aren't looking. Always good if it's a store that sells clothes – find the biggest bras you can and plop them in their trolley amongst the groceries. FUNNY.

NOTE: Funnier if you put a bra in a man's trolley. Obviously.

● ●

JANUARY 23RD

Are you bad at making decisions? When your mind is very anxious, indecision can be crippling. Here's an idea to free you up.

Go to a café or restaurant. Pick up the menu, close your eyes and point to something. You HAVE to have that!

JANUARY 24TH

Is your mind racing? Lots of worries? Feeling unsettled? Well, know they are just thoughts, they are not real and nor do they define you. They will pass.

Get some balloons. As you blow them up, blow your worries into them. Once you have a number of balloons blown up, have a good muck about, hitting them, kicking them, playing tennis or volleyball with them. Then decide it's time to release all the worries and pop the hell out of them all. And relax.

• •

JANUARY 25TH

Do you ever feel shy walking into a room, crowded or otherwise? Feel like you shouldn't take up too much space? Well, remember you are a brilliant, unique person and the world needs you to be freely who you are.

Today go about making fabulous entrances. Stop in a doorway adopting a pose, hands resting on the frame. Sweep in like Beyoncé. Announce your arrival spectacularly.

NOTE: I once heard someone say that beautiful means "be you to the full". I love that.

JANUARY 26TH

Struggling with body image? I have a possible solution today.

Watch Cameron Russell's TED Talk called 'Looks aren't everything. Believe me, I'm a model'. IT'S AMAZING. It's only 10 minutes long and just might change your perspective forever.

● ●

JANUARY 27TH

The grown-up, embarrassed adult in you might be resisting finding the time for your inner child to play. But you know you want to. You know it's good for you.

Run down a hill (or any gradient you can find) and shout 'Weeeeeeee!' You could get on a bike, a skateboard (even if you sit on it and treat it like a toboggan), dust off those roller skates, or just skip down a hill.

NOTE: If you are over 35 and running, I hope you are just saying 'Weeeeee' and not actually weeing. A trip to the toilet before you begin any kind of skipping might be advisable. (Just me?!)

JANUARY 28TH

Email is a wonderful invention but nothing beats a hand-written letter.

Write someone a little card encouraging them by saying why you value them. Or, better, give a letter to the postman – it could just say, 'I am giving you a letter to say how excellent you are at giving letters. Have a wonderful day.'

Oh, go on, the postie will LOVE IT.

● ●

JANUARY 29TH

Pets are such life-affirmers. Really pay attention to your beloved animal today. Let them remind you how loved you are. And how in the moment they are – not worrying or projecting ahead like we constantly do.

Do a filmic pose with your pet – try Lady and the Tramp *with a long piece of spaghetti between you and your dog! Anyone going to do a* Ghost *style pottery shot with their rabbit? I want photos people!*

NOTE: If you don't have a pet, get thee to funny animal YouTube clips. Oh the joys.

JANUARY 30TH

It's important to celebrate. Not just birthdays or big moments, but small daily achievements, too. You are doing amazingly, so celebrate yourself.

Do an over-the-top goal celebration for a tiny task, like putting something in a bin. Goal celebrations include running or sliding to an imaginary corner flag and soaking up the applause, doing the Peter Crouch robot, or putting your shirt over your head and running around the room!

NOTE: I favour the classic Tennis fist pump celebration pose.

• •

JANUARY 31ST

A fun idea to wake you up this morning or try it at the end of day to let out any irritations you may need to release.

AIR DRUM! Air drum away. If you need a song recommendation, I'd go with Phil Collins In the Air Tonight! If you are air drumming at the end of the day, drum with vigour, let all the day's woes fall away via the classic air drum manoeuvre.

NOTE: If January has been difficult for any reason, drum it away, tomorrow is a new day and a new month. Tell yourself life is on the up. Because it really can be. You are doing brilliantly, even if it doesn't feel that way. Don't criticize yourself unnecessarily, you wouldn't do it to a friend, be kind to YOU.

FEBRUARY

FEBRUARY 1ST

Happy February to you and you and you. Let's start the fresh new month by really breaking any sense of boredom or routine.

Get a map of your area, close your eyes, and point to somewhere on the map. Go there! SUCH FUN.

NOTE: You might need to limit the area of the map in order to achieve this. Do NOT get a globe out! Unless you are feeling particularly free, adventurous and flush.

FEBRUARY 2ND

As Olivia Newton John would say, 'Let's get physical.' Happy body, happy mind. But let's not jog because, as you may know, I don't approve of running, unless done professionally or as a child.

Fashion some maracas. If you don't have actual maracas can I suggest filling a couple of empty water bottles with rice. Or even just grab a wooden spoon and get maraca-ing. Get those arms moving. Shake those maracas (not a euphemism).

NOTE: I have a fitness video available called *Maracattack* (no, really) and it has a great 20-minute routine for cardio, amongst other fun ways to get fit.

● ●

FEBRUARY 3RD

A very silly thought for today. But, as I will regularly remind you, this book-ette is about releasing joy to push out the negative. So: teachers are meant to have teachers' pets, right?

Bring a teacher a pet. Probably not a real one – though, that would be funny. Maybe a toy. Or even a fruit friend. Something he or she can call a pet. Teacher's pet. Brilliant.

NOTE: If you don't have connections to schools/teachers, then why not google an old teacher, see what they are up to and indeed look like now (always intriguing). Or Facebook them and send them a photo of a pet. Or get in touch with an old school friend and remember a teacher together.

FEBRUARY 4TH

It may be a scary notion but we need to express those pent-up emotions. It's important to check in with what's going on inside. Are you feeling a little wound up, perhaps a bit angry?

Throw something with gay abandon! A pillow. A toy. A cat (joke). Fill a balloon with water and throw it against a wall or smash it on the ground.

Have a good old throw. Let it all out.

• •

FEBRUARY 5TH

Feeling fed up with the long, dark nights? Here's another way to make a dreary winter night a Such Fun Event . . . OWLS!

Go on a night-time adventure. Drive or walk to your nearest countryside and see if you can hear an OWL. Nothing more lovely than a 'twit twoo'!

NOTE: If you can't do this, or you try and have no success, have a google for Cute Owl Videos. They are amazing beasts. Perhaps try your own owl impersonation.

FEBRUARY 6TH

We all have people who inspire us. I don't believe in obsessive celebrity idolizing, as such, but there have always been amazing people (famous or not) who have gone before us in history who we can draw inspiration from. If it weren't for my comedy hero Eric Morecambe, I wouldn't have been inspired by the world of comedy.

Change a photo in a frame in the house to someone your family member loves. Maybe put loads of them about. Put one on their pillow! And/or think of the person who inspires you, read some quotes you love about them, find out more about them, do something that emulates their attributes.

● ●

FEBRUARY 7TH

Get filmic. Adding a heightened film scenario into your day might stop things feeling mundane. Keep the mind stimulated.

Act out a scene from a film. On your own or with a friend. Any film you love. The final scene of Casablanca, *maybe, or the top of the Empire State building in* Sleepless in Seattle.

My choice would probably be a musical – Dirty Dancing *anyone?*

FEBRUARY 8TH

Sometimes we need to push ourselves a little to feel we've achieved something we thought we couldn't do. Anxiety doesn't want you to feel empowered. But empowered you must be, because you can do way more than you think you can.

Somersault on the bed!

Added fun if you do it with no prior warning to a partner lying next to you.

• •

FEBRUARY 9TH

Need to spice up life in the bedroom department but not necessarily in the sex (MOUTH IT, we're British) way.

Buy a remote control fart machine or get a fart app or a whoppee cushion. Set it off. HILARIOUS.

NOTE: If you don't find farting funny, I can but apologize. Equally, though: WHAT'S WRONG WITH YOU?!

FEBRUARY 10TH

We are designed for relationships. Relationships with friends and loved ones bring extraordinary joy and purpose to our lives. Connection is vital for a healthy nervous system. But relationships can go wrong. This is a bit of a tough one today but it's important, so have a mull.

Think about a broken relationship that needs mending. Can you forgive, put it behind you, give them a call and go and do something fun together? Is there a bad feeling with a friend you need to air? Is there someone particularly tricky and demanding, who take, take, takes? Don't step back but find a way to create boundaries for yourself whilst staying loving. Don't let the sun go down today on any anger, as I believe the saying goes.

● ●

FEBRUARY 11TH

Even household chores that get you down can be jollied up.

Do the ironing while listening to the song Under Pressure *by Queen. Sing it to the clothes as you put them under "ironing" pressure. Do you see? Fun.*

FEBRUARY 12TH

Some days just feel grey, eh? RHYME. Especially in February.
Today I declare to be FIESTA DAY!

*Go as big or small as you dare. You could just say 'hola' to
someone at work or go the whole hog and have a party at
home. Fiesta music, grass skirts, do some hula, maracas, cook
fajitas – go fiesta. Have a spin in your Ford Fiesta with fiesta
music blaring, if you are lucky enough to own a Fiesta. Happy
FIESTA Day!*

· ·

FEBRUARY 13TH

It's good to think of others – makes you feel better about
yourself as you think beyond your own problems. You can go
to sleep knowing today you were kind to someone. You get
less anxious and frazzled and kinder. Win, win.

*Say to someone, 'You make the world a better place because
there is only one of you. So, hurrah for you!' and give them a
round of applause.*

FEBRUARY 14TH

I am not a fan of St Valentine's Day. As I said once in my sitcom, 'I don't know much about St Valentine but I hope he died alone surrounded by couples!' To make a romantic gesture on a commercial day when you *have* to do so doesn't feel romantic to me. But, hey, spread the love today, in case you meet people who are alone.

Buy some single flowers and scatter them around – give them to people at the bus stop, put them on people's desks and on doorsteps. Spread the love.

● ●

FEBRUARY 15TH

February can be a difficult month. The strongest of us can succumb to the winter blues. Here's a thought.

GET OUT ALL YOUR CHRISTMAS DECORATIONS AGAIN! Put up fairy lights, bung on a Santa hat, put some tinsel up. Make the house feel sparkly again for a few days/or indeed until the end of winter. No rules here, I say.

FEBRUARY 16TH

Instead of wishing winter away, try and embrace and find the joy in it.

Have a roast in a pub. Make a cottage pie. Put your pyjamas on the minute you get home, snuggle up and watch TV. Embrace the things you wouldn't do in the summer. Have a hot bath in the middle of the day. Yum.

NOTE: My personal favourite winter embrace is getting in a sleeping bag or inside a duvet and shuffling about the house like a geisha, only removing it when absolutely necessary.

●●●●●●●●●●●●●●●●●●●●●●●●●●●●●●●

FEBRUARY 17TH

Remember the body likes to be in movement, it unlocks the mind and frees you emotionally. It is always harder to get moving in the winter. Here's an idea that might help.

Awaken your soul with a skip or two today. A quick skip down the street. Or an actual skip with a rope. And definitely, at least once, skip to the loo singing, 'Skip, skip, skip to the loo. Skip, skip, skip to the loo. Skip, skip, skip to the loo. Skip to the loo, my darling.'

FEBRUARY 18TH

We don't dress for dinner any more as a society. We rarely dress up. Which, frankly, I am fine with – I'd happily wear tracksuit bottoms and slippers every day. But might it be fun this evening to . . .

Dress up for dinner. Or simply, just wear a hat. Any hat. Just bung on a hat. Make a hat out of foil. Make your meal a 'hat meal'. Or wear three hats throughout the meal – HAT TRICK. Get it? I am HILARIOUS.

● ●

FEBRUARY 19TH

Children's books are blooming lovely aren't they? Simple and gentle. Let's have a moment today to make life uncomplicated again.

If you are lucky enough to live near a bridge and stream, like Christopher Robin, have a game of Pooh sticks. If not, enjoy my favourite Winnie the Pooh quotes below. I hope they warm the cockles of your heart like they do mine.

'What day is it?' 'It's today,' squeaked Piglet. 'My favourite day,' said Pooh.

'Rivers know this: there is no hurry. We shall get there one day.'

'The things that make me different are the things that make me, ME.'

'Supposing a tree fell down, Pooh, when we were underneath it,' said Piglet. 'Supposing it didn't,' said Pooh. After careful thought Piglet was comforted by this.

FEBRUARY 20TH

Are you feeling tired? Flagging a bit? Want some more energy?

You must BOUNCE! Trampoline? Space hopper? Bed? Or just bounce up and down for a bit in the office or at home. Try a group bounce. Get that energy flowing. BOUNCE AWAY.

Disclaimer: As ever, men and women over 35, please do a wee before bouncing.

● ●

FEBRUARY 21ST

I declare this to be EGG DAY! Don't get to BOILing point, or SCRAMBLE yourself with worries so you CRACK. This can be an EGGcellent day, despite all you are going through. Please applaud my egg word play. Thank you!

Have boiled eggs and soldiers. Or scramble them and have them on lovely buttered toast. Maybe paint some eggs or felt tip a smiley face on to them. Have a fun moment with an egg basically! You could put all your eggs in one basket, for example. More hilarious egg word play there. You're welcome.

FEBRUARY 22ND

Need to dissipate some tricky vibes in the household?

Learn the EastEnders *drum routine. If someone leaves the room in a huff, grab some makeshift drumsticks (wooden spoons, forks, even chicken drumsticks) and do the dramatic sound effect.*

●●●●●●●●●●●●●●●●●●●●●●●●●●●●●●●

FEBRUARY 23RD

Shopping can be enjoyable for some. For others it's a chore (personally, I am not a fan). But I know it can be jollied up for today's Daily Dose of Such Fun.

Do a blindfold purchase. Blindfold a friend. Be their escort in the supermarket, chemist, bookshop (wherever you decide to go) as they choose to buy something. You have to get what they lay their hands on! Maybe you can give it to someone as a gift.

FEBRUARY 24TH

Healthy eating is so important to emotional well-being (especially reducing sugars). We are what we eat. But I also believe in treating ourselves occasionally, especially in winter. Everything in moderation. I go by the 80/20 rule. Eighty per cent healthy, 20 per cent nice treats.

Today is PIE DAY! Let's have a pie. What's your favourite? Are you going to have a sweet pie? Or a savoury pie? Are you going to be on your own or savour your pie with someone else? Whatever you do, ENJOY A PIE!

● ●

FEBRUARY 25TH

The world is an unequal place. We are safe and not hungry most of the time. But our fellow humans, only a few hours' plane journey away, are in great and grave need.

Donate what you feel you can to a charity that provides shelter, food, clean water or medical support to those most in need. E.g. Tearfund, WaterAid, Comic Relief.

FEBRUARY 26TH

We all know the pressure of a never-ending To Do list. But do you ever celebrate what you have got done rather than look at what you have yet to do?

Make a TA DA list! Pop on Heather Small's **What Have You Done Today To Make You Feel Proud***? and make a Ta Da list of all the things you have done, however small they may be, and shout them out. YOU'RE AMAZING.*

• •

FEBRUARY 27TH

As I mentioned last month, singing is great for the soul – opens up your airways, gets you breathing nice and deep.

Sing really loudly in the bath or shower or car. Or bus stop, if you dare. Channel your inner Mariah or Whitney. If you've got an iPod or smartphone with music, put in your headphones, but sing along in public, as loudly as you like. Add in some moves and sing your heart out!

FEBRUARY 28TH

Don't you hate queues? SO frustrating. But today, you can bring cheer to them.

Learn The Full Monty *dance routine, and start doing it with a friend or two in a queue while singing along. It will make you happy and make those around you laugh too.*

NOTE: I am not suggesting doing the FULL Monty and stripping in public. Just the routine. Thank you!

● ●

FEBRUARY 29TH

That means it's a LEAP YEAR! So . . .

Today – LEAP. That's it. Just leap as much as you can. Leap in as many different ways as you can find possible. Game of leap-frog perhaps? I want to see some adults leapfrogging for the first time in decades. Happy Leaping!

MARCH

● ●

MARCH 1ST

Happy 1st March to you. Today is about MARCHING – obviously! Are mornings always chaotic in your house? Is getting yourself or everyone out of the door making you feel like a crazed animal, running from one thing to the next?

Put on some Military Marching Band music and march your way out of the door. Shout orders like a sergeant. Expect a 'Yes, sir' back. Military precision this morning. You could of course have eggs and SOLDIERS. And why not keep marching down the street. MARCH. Because it's MARCH!

MARCH 2ND

Simple changes to your appearance can make you feel different, and give you a fresh spring in your step. What about a new hair cut?.

Why don't you and a friend cut each other's hair. Oh go on!

NOTE: avoid (or embrace if you're very brave) the pudding bowl cut. My mother did it to me regularly in the 70's. I looked like a cross between a monk and Anne Widdicombe, aged 7.

● ●

MARCH 3RD

Have a mull on this: we are often not very good at meeting our needs. We sometimes don't even know what our needs are, or we just spend too much time meeting other peoples'.

Bravely state a need. I'll start: 'I just need half an hour to myself, so please respect that and give me the time and space to regain my energy.'

NOTE: That's quite a useful one if you are desperate to go and fart. There's nothing worse than trapped wind.

MARCH 4TH

Carrying on from meeting our needs yesterday: we often worry we will upset someone or we feel bad for stating our own needs and wants.

Put on Billy Joel's My Life. *Have a good expressive dance and tell yourself it's your life, you can do what you want to do with it, and it's important to meet your own needs to live life to the full.*

A quote I like from Harvey Fierstein: "Accept no one's definition of your life; define yourself."

● ●

MARCH 5TH

Don't you love a holiday? Especially a holiday in a hotel. I do LOVE a hotel room. Mini kettle, sachet drinks, and complimentary biscuits anyone?

Give your loved ones a hotel turn-down service. Make their bed in a delicious way, put the lamp on, turn the duvet down, put their slippers by the side of the bed, and put a chocolate on their pillow. And how about writing out a breakfast menu and making them breakfast in bed the next morning.

NOTE: For additional amusement you could print out the weather forecast for the next day and put too many pillows and cushions on the bed. Get as hotel-y (new word) as you like.

MARCH 6TH

Let's extend the hotel theme from yesterday and spread the love even further.

Every time you use a toilet today (and you can even go to some public ones, you don't need to use them to do this), rearrange the toilet roll into a hotel style pointy tip. How nice for the next person! SUCH FUN.

● ●

MARCH 7TH

It's often easy to feel out of control. But you are in control of how you spend your time and your key life decisions. Today is a light way to remind you of that.

Before you need to switch on a light, say 'Let there be light' and ceremoniously switch it on. You controlled that light switch. You ARE in control. As I once said in my sitcom, 'If I'd be better, I'd be God'!

MARCH 8TH

We should chat more to strangers – we're all together on this planet, so let's commune with people. Looking beyond ourselves can really help reduce our anxiety, and remind us we aren't the only ones in pain. The more generous we are, despite having a bad day, the lighter our day will become.

Go up to people today and say, 'Do you know the way to San Jose?' FUNNY! And it might just start a marvellous conversation.

Thank you, dear Bella, for this suggestion.

● ●

MARCH 9TH

If you smile, even a fake smile, it has a positive effect on your nervous system. It coaxes your mind and body to switch off the stress state you might be in.

SMILE TODAY! Smile at strangers, at shopkeepers, at wait-resses. Just crack a smile wherever you go. Spread the joy. And make yourself feel better at the same time.

MARCH 10TH

A varied diet is important to get lots of lovely nutrients into your system in order to make it work as beautifully as it can.

Try and eat something you have never eaten before. It's about a NEW TASTE.

I'll start: I am going to have game. I've never had pheasant before. I know – hark at me, living like a character out of **Downton Abbey** *for the day.*

NOTE: Where on EARTH do I get a pheasant?! You may want to pluck (PUN) for something easier. Like papaya perhaps. Or okra (what IS that?).

● ●

MARCH 11TH

Sometimes we just need to feel a little cheeky.

Have you ever gone commando? I dare you for a day. How does it feel to be at work with no one knowing YOU HAVE NO PANTS ON!

NOTE: Please don't wear a skirt on a windy day. Good luck.

MARCH 12TH

Do you get bored with your clothes and find yourself wearing the same things every day? Remember, breaking our habits is a key remedy for anxiety and stress busting.

Wear a colourful scarf with gay abandon today. Swish it like a movie star. Put it in a turban. Let your scarf make you feel fabulously beautiful and elegant. BECAUSE YOU ARE.

NOTE: If you just said to yourself, 'But, Miranda, I'm not beautiful' give yourself a little slap on the hands. Naughty self-criticizing you! Be kind to yourself.

●●●●●●●●●●●●●●●●●●●●●●●●●●●●●●●

MARCH 13TH

Do you ever feel less clever than others? I do. We can have fun changing that feeling.

Put your favourite magazine – even if it's **The Beano** *– inside* **The Spectator** *or* **The Economist** *and read it on the tube or train. Or your favourite book inside a copy of* War and Peace*!*

MARCH 14TH

I never used to read much; I was too restless and thought it was boring. Plus, I enjoy television more as a medium for storytelling. But we can learn so much from books, poetry and plays. And they can be a good place to start exploring emotions. In our wonderful world of constant availability to television, let's not forget literature.

Read a poem, or a Shakespeare sonnet, or start a book you have never read – a classic, maybe. Savour the language. Perhaps read it out loud to friends or family by candlelight, pretending it's a couple of centuries ago. Imagine you are courting Mr Darcy as you read!

● ●

MARCH 15TH

Don't you just LOVE tea? I LOVE tea. Ooh, tea is SO GOOD. The simple act of making tea can go a long way.

Choose someone today you are going to make and have a cup of tea with. I suggest also singing 'Tea for two' whilst making it. If you're embarrassed, just say, "Miranda told me to!" Do a lovely mug chink with a hearty "Cheers" before you drink it. Really savour your tea break. Tea . . . yum . . .

MARCH 16TH

Spring is in the air. Spring is a time of hope and joy and new life. Even if circumstances tell you otherwise, things can change, so don't fear the future, just think about and try and enjoy today.

Pick or buy two flowers, keep one for yourself and give one to a stranger saying, 'Welcome to spring. Have a lovely day because you are lovely.'

● ●

MARCH 17TH

We all feel alone sometimes. Even if we have good family and friends. Often what we go through is very personal and no one can really ever understand it.

Really let yourself go. Feel sad and low, let it all out, have a healing weep – bung on All By Myself *and GO FOR IT! This is your brief "pity party". Now, dry your eyes, and call a friend to remind yourself that everyone is battling something.*

NOTE: If you don't feel up to speaking to someone then treat yourself to an episode of your favourite TV show or a chapter of your favourite book. I find the characters can feel like friends.

MARCH 18TH

A challenge that might help you connect with your fellow humans. Remember we are all in this thing called life together. And at the risk of sounding like your mother, there are real people out there; they aren't all on social media.

Wink at 17 people today.

NOTE: Not creepy pervy winks! Just friendly smiley ones. You never know, you may find the love of your life.

● ●

MARCH 19TH

Are you rushing again? We are always SO busy. Try and reduce hurry in your life. But if you are in an unavoidable rush . . .

Adopt an amusing emergency walk – a fast half-walk half-run to avoid a jog. Get those hips wiggling. Make it as eccentric as you like. You might as well enjoy being in a rush.

MARCH 20TH

Receiving a gift is such a wonderful feeling – it makes you feel special and appreciated. And getting a gift on a random day for no reason? Even better.

If you have a spare fiver, tenner, or couple of quid, go with a friend or loved one to a poundshop and buy two, five or ten silly gifts for each other. Present them ceremoniously wrapped or unwrapped.

● ●

MARCH 21ST

Yesterday I suggested random gift giving to your loved ones. Today let's take this idea one step even further.

Buy a gift, however big or small you can afford (there's nothing wrong with something worth 50p), and give it to a stranger you think needs cheering up. Say, 'Hi, you look a bit sad, I hope you're not, but here's a gift in case you are.' Remember, you can always say, 'Miranda told me to do it,' if they look at you strangely!

MARCH 22ND

I am not a fan of gyms. I'll say it again, they SMELL OF CROTCH. And fresh air is such a key part of exercise for me. If you like the gym but find your workout repetitive, then here's an idea to liven it up.

Get two yoga balls in a row on some mats. Take a little run up. Dive on top of them so you roll along, your stomach on one, legs on another. SUCH FUN.

NOTE: I have also done this with large rolls of bubble wrap in an office!

● ●

MARCH 23RD

Don't be down on your looks. Oh no, no, no, don't you go doing that again. I will keep reminding you that you are the ONLY person on earth who looks like you. So, you are AMAZING.

Look in the mirror and say to yourself with as much conviction as you can muster, 'I am utterly unique, there is only one of me and therefore I am totally beautiful. Well done me, I ROCK!'

NOTE: I think we should say this to ourselves at least once a day. And any thoughts you have like, 'I'm too fat' or 'Other people are prettier' – they are just thoughts. Not the truth.

MARCH 24TH

Let's have a little morning perk up, if you pardon the expression. It involves the musical *Singing in the Rain*. I think it is a wonderfully life-affirming film and one of the best musicals of all time.

Put on Good Morning *from* Singing in the Rain. *Sing a loving 'Good Morning' to whoever you live with to feel renewed appreciation for them.*

NOTE: The dance routine to this from the musical is utterly wonderful. Perhaps watch it around the breakfast table. Maybe even attempt to copy it.

• •

MARCH 25TH

Want to feel a bit more passionate? Us Brits aren't great at passion, are we? Some of us even find the word sexual, a bit, well, sexual. But it's important to get in touch with our inner passion.

Grab someone and do a tango move or two. You know that cheek to cheek walk through a room, dramatic turn and back again. You could always add in putting a rose in your teeth. Or have a look online for a tango class. GET TANGO-ING.

Today is TANGO DAY!

MARCH 26TH

To break the habit of not saying hello to strangers, or even our neighbours (us Londoners are particularly bad about that), how about using a friendly, gung-ho 'Yo' to your fellow humans today? But let's make it Miranda-esque and add in a dollop of random fun.

Buy a cheap yo-yo (a much underrated pastime). Go up to a friend, or a stranger if you're feeling brave, and greet them with a hearty, 'Yo!' Whip out your yo-yo (not a euphemism), add another 'Yo' and start playing with your yo-yo (definitely not a euphemism).

NOTE: If nothing else, suddenly trying to be skilled at the yo-yo will distract your mind from any nasty fearful thoughts.

• •

MARCH 27TH

Want to feel a bit more magical?

Learn a magic trick. SIMPLE!

NOTE: Or, if you have a dog, you could try and teach it some tricks. Then you can say, 'I have taught an old dog new tricks.' I really am HILARIOUS.

MARCH 28TH

Easter approach-eth (medieval-esque speech – you're welcome).

Why is it just the kids who get to make an Easter bonnet? How about teachers, too? Make one for them. Suggest Easter bonnet competitions in your workplace. Make one for yourself – Happy Bonnet Day! (Lovely word – BONNET.)

● ●

MARCH 29TH

Easter is all about new life, new beginnings, fresh starts. (And chocolate.)

Say this to yourself out loud at least three times today: 'I let the past be past, at last. I forgive myself and leave all the hurt behind me. I am a new creation.'

I have this poem on my kitchen wall to look at every day: "Don't look back in to the past, what was fire is now ash, let it all be dead and gone, the time is now for moving on."

MARCH 30TH

Too often we feel dowdy and unglamorous. Looks are by no means the important part of us; we are working on our inner selves BUT it is important to feel happy in our own skin and body. It's the only body we have, let's feel good in it and treat it well.

Go to a department store. Go to the perfume counter. Spray some scent ahead of you and then walk into it like a chic Parisian! Then walk out of the store on to the street with the song Pretty Woman *playing in your head (ideally tee it up on your phone and listen to it) and strut like the glamourpuss you are. Or if you are brave enough, sing or play it out loud as you strut. Strut away. You are worthy of a strut. You are a beautiful strutter.*

NOTE: Men may want to play or sing *It's Raining Men*. Nice.

• •

MARCH 31ST

The clocks must have recently gone forward so . . .

Do the TIME WARP. You know the one from The Rocky Horror Show. *Put it on and DO THE DANCE! Dance into the freedom of spring and those longer nights ahead.*

APRIL

● ●

APRIL 1ST

It's April Fool's Day! But as this book is entirely about being
silly and foolish for our improved mental health, today . . .

*Our April Fool is to be serious! Have a day where you may
want to reflect, debate, get a bit philosophical, or spiritual. Ask
searching questions. It might lead to an interesting debate.
Today you can sort out the meaning of life whilst everyone else
is being foolish.*

APRIL 2ND

Yesterday was serious, so let's get back on track with a simple idea to jolly life up with random silliness.

Eat a spaghetti dish with your hands tied behind your back!

●●●●●●●●●●●●●●●●●●●●●●●●●●●●●●●●●

APRIL 3RD

We often think we need to work our problems out, analyze them, try and find the solutions. But, actually, sometimes we just need to surrender and stop trying to fix things.

Instead of working out your and other people's problems, try and solve some fun problems. How about a jigsaw? Sudoku? Crossword? You could play some Scrabble. Or find some Brain Teasers online. Solve some other problems and yours might fade away or, indeed, answers might start coming to you as you relax your mind.

APRIL 4TH

Technology is of course a wonderful thing. However, one downside is that it can reduce family time and community spirit. Social media can't compete with the laughs had in a room with a group of close friends or family.

Have an Old-fashioned Parlour Games Day or Evening. Charades anyone? The hat game is one of my favourites. Play games and enjoy the ensuing larks. There are larks to be had people, LARKS! Repeat after me: 'Larks!' Lovely. Even saying larks brings larks. I've said larks too much now. LARKS.

● ●

APRIL 5TH

Yesterday I enjoyed the word larks. I love words. If you know me well, I believe the queen of all words, because it's ghastly and joyful in equal measure and most certainly fun to say, is MOIST. The king of all words is PLINTH. And my favourite word to say is:

PLUNGE! Today enjoy saying the word PLUNGE. Say it as often as you dare and wish to. 'Oooh, I must just PLUNGE into that shop.' 'I am going to PLUNGE into my lunch.' 'Wouldn't you just love to PLUNGE into a PLUNGE pool?'

APRIL 6TH

As you know by now, I like to jolly up home life, particularly those daily mundane tasks. This will be a good one if you happen to be gearing up for a spring clean.

As you clear up the kitchen after a meal today, or whilst you're cooking, have a group sing-a-long using as many kitchen utensils as possible as microphones. Whisks, spoons, work it with the masher!

● ●

APRIL 7TH

Is the bedroom department getting a bit stale?

Find some animal noises online. Line them up to play on your phone. Just as your partner is getting into bed, press play. Give them the fright of their life as there will suddenly be a lion roaring, or an owl hooting! SUCH FUN.

NOTE: You never know this may end up making you feel a bit more animal in other ways. CHEEKY.

APRIL 8TH

I am a big fan of power naps. Taking 10 or 20 minutes out of the day to slow down, take some deep breaths, hopefully fall asleep and recharge. Don't feel guilty about it. It's good for you.

Take a pillow with you to work and lie down under your desk/ at the school gate/in your lecture/on your boss's desk and have a little nap.

NOTE: I once made a pillow out of Jiffy bags and a mattress out of bubble wrap and had a little sleep in the stationery cupboard at work. I worked much better afterwards!

● ●

APRIL 9TH

I LOVE stationery. I used to be an office manager and was in charge of all stationery ordering. I would refuse to let some dreary days at the office get me down. Admin needn't be dull.

Make a bulldog clip tower. Or a necklace out of paperclips. Having regular breaks from your work makes you more productive, so get creative with stationery.

APRIL 10TH

We all need to eat more fruit and veg. It's easy to go a few days and not get our five or more a day.

Buy some pineapples and some oranges. Before you make a smoothie, GET BOWLING. See if the oranges can knock those pineapples over.

NOTE: Permission granted to substitute the fruit suggestions, though you may struggle to roll a banana.

● ●

APRIL 11TH

Still on the healthy body theme today. We are made up of water. We are told to drink 1.5 to 2 litres of water a day. We all need water to survive. However, not everyone in the world has access to clean water.

Today, simply appreciate water. Watch it come out of the tap, feel it, enjoy the sensation of quenching your thirst. Put a slice of lemon in it and some ice. Bring someone a lovely glass of water. Splash someone with a bit of water. Throw a glass of water in someone's face, if it's appropriate! Pour a glass of water over your head. Have a long bath. Enjoy the feel o' water.

APRIL 12TH

Remember, freeing up your body is really key to emotional health. When your body feels you are relaxing, it can reduce muscle tension and send positive messages to your nervous system.

Today, bung on some classical music and get the family doing ballet around the living area. Nothing funnier than attempting ballet, especially when you have NO IDEA how to do it. Get your nan doing some moves, too. Even the dog. Let's BALLET!

NOTE: It's actually very amusing, I have discovered, to do ballet moves to non-classical music. Bung on Beiber and ballet (which is also to fun to say).

● ●

APRIL 13TH

Want to challenge your inner maverick? Oh yeah, you can be maverick.

At one meal today, go sweet BEFORE savoury. Pudding first anyone? WOW! MAVERICK.

APRIL 14TH

I have explained that community is important for a calm nervous system, and extending that further, so is physical contact.

Today is the day to GIVE LOTS OF HUGS. Obviously where appropriate. Running up to and hugging a policeman might be a bit weird. But, hey, you could try. They aren't going to arrest you for being nice!

• •

APRIL 15TH

We are at the heart of spring. This can only mean one thing. It's time for our joy-filled seasonal SPRING GALLOP!

Gallop in a public place today at LEAST once. Just break into a gallop – see if you can get anyone to join in. Gallop across a zebra crossing, perhaps.

NOTE: As ever, neighing noises, the use of an imaginary whip, and other horse-based mimes are wholly encouraged.

APRIL 16TH

Mary Poppins is a great filmic example of providing structure and joy into a previously chaotic household.

Put on Let's Go Fly A Kite *from* Mary Poppins *and have a sing-a-long. If you have a kite, go and fly it. If you don't, plan when you could buy or make one. It might be really fun. Let's All Go Fly A Kite.*

NOTE: Remember any songs you may not know will be on YouTube.

●●●●●●●●●●●●●●●●●●●●●●●●●●●●●

APRIL 17TH

Do you have to cook for your family and you're tired of it? Do you live alone and don't want to cook for yourself? Do you, like me, just struggle to love cooking?

Welcome to MAKE A CRAZY PUDDING DAY. Throw some crazy random ingredients you love into a Magimix and make an eccentric mousse. Ice cream with Maltesers, an orange, some jelly – I mean, WHY NOT? Anything goes.

APRIL 18TH

Today I am suggesting you learn a poem. Or a line from a poem. I have always envied people with good memories who can quote sayings and poems. And it is much better to fill our minds with wonderful poetry than the usual drip-feed of fearful or anxious thoughts.

Wander about your office, school, or home in the style of a poet (perhaps bung on a quirky hat, even a beret) and when you find an appropriate moment, say, 'That reminds me of that poem . . .' and quote it in the style of a literary genius. Then swan out. Love your style!

● ●

APRIL 19TH

Today let's think about our little feathered friends: birds and ducks. They never know where their next meal is coming from or what each day will hold, but they don't sit on branches having breakdowns in a state of terrible anxiety! They just do peacefully what they can and need to do.

Go and feed some birds or ducks. Watch how free and happy they are pecking away at this exciting treat. Be in the moment as you freely watch them being in the moment – what a gorgeous circle that is.

NOTE: Apparently bread isn't good for ducks. So ideally try and find some seeds. Spread the word. And, talking Mary Poppins as we were a few days ago, don't hold back from singing *Feed the Birds* if the mood takes you today.

APRIL 20TH

Love makes the world go around. All you need is love. Love is all you need.

Call everyone today 'darling' or 'my love' or 'honey'. And mean it sincerely with, well, love. Don't laugh at others, love at others.

● ●

APRIL 21ST

Today we continue the love theme. To quote Wet Wet Wet: 'Love is all around us. It's everywhere we go.' You could always put that song on to start your day. And let's make sure love is all around us.

Send as many people as you can a loving text. It can be the same one to everyone, or you could personalize them. A nice thing to do on your commute, or at a time when you usually check emails or play a game on your phone. Tell people you love them or how special they are.

APRIL 22ND

If you haven't heard of Brené Brown, she is an amazing woman I would like to introduce you to – she is a social scientist who has researched many things about what makes us happier.

Watch Brené Brown's 'The Power of Vulnerability' on YouTube. IT'S A-M-A-ZING.

When people ask you how you are today, don't just say, 'I'm fine' if you really aren't. Risk being vulnerable. Say, for example, 'I'm having a tough time, but it will be ok. You?' It leads to open conversations and makes people feel better about themselves.

● ●

APRIL 23RD

Mornings are my worst time. Anyone else? They can be tough. I usually wake up more tired than when I went to sleep. Groggy and horrid. And often a little down. Here's a Such Fun antidote.

Put on Dolly Parton's 9 to 5 before you get out of bed. Sing along and act out as many of the lyrics as you can. Yawn and stretch and try and come to life.

APRIL 24TH

Are you feeling ill? Got a cold or have a longer-term health problem? Or do you just feel vulnerable for no particular reason and need some comfort? That morning feeling again

Lie on top of your duvet. Hold one end of it and roll. Put yourself into a DUVET COCOON. SNUG FUN.

● ●

APRIL 25TH

Is it raining? Those dratted April Showers. Don't worry — fun shall still be had. And you can do this today come rain or shine.

Do some of the steps from Singing in the Rain. *Hop up and down along the pavement, swing around a lamppost, have a jump in a puddle.*

NOTE: If you don't know the routine, search for *Singing in the Rain* and Gene Kelly on YouTube. And if it's *really* raining and you haven't seen the film, snuggle up and WATCH IT!

APRIL 26TH

Yesterday I mentioned *Singing in the Rain*, as I have before (a little obsessed). Well, just to help remind us why we are trying to do a dollop of Such Fun a day . . .

Watch the Make 'Em Laugh *routine from* Singing in the Rain. *It will perk you up around the breakfast table. It's an amazing performance by Donald O'Connor and maybe you can try one of his steps today.*

Our aim every day is to make the world a jollier place for ourselves and others. This will remind you to Make 'em Laugh. I told you *Singing in the Rain* was brilliant.

● ●

APRIL 27TH

Hopefully this should make you and others laugh today.

Go to a café and order a drink (it has to be a place where they will require your name for the order) and, when they ask, choose a crazy name like Queen/King FlippetyMop or Prince/ Princess of Spongeland. Or, if you are a woman, call yourself Keith and, if a man, plump for Audrey. It will make the person making the coffee and the person who has to read it out laugh. And hopefully the people queuing, too.

APRIL 28TH

Following on from the strange name jollity of yesterday . . .

Choose a name you would like to be called today. Make it clear to those around you and refuse to answer to anything else. If you get to meet someone today for the first time I dare you to introduce yourself with your fictional name. Example names: Cinderella, Prince Charming, Harry Potter, Mrs George Clooney, Mr Cameron Diaz. As ever, anything goes.

● ●

APRIL 29TH

Ever feel like you deserve some royal treatment? You should do, you're amazing. Don't go forgetting that now, will you? I will have no beating yourself up on my watch!

Pretend to be the Queen at least once during the day today. In whatever ways you wish. I suggest when in a car, taxi or bus that you do a royal wave to passers-by. You could also use the word 'one' a lot. 'One is going to make a cup of tea. One would happily make it for others, even though one is the Queen.'

APRIL 30TH

It's the 30th April. Which means it's the 1st May tomorrow. I know, don't say you don't learn from me. I often forget to make the most of May and June, thinking summer is a way off, but they are often the best months, with the longest evenings. I am giving you tomorrow's task in advance.

Set your alarm in time to go and see the sunrise. Either from your house or, if you live near a hill or at the top of a block, head there. Have a kip today if you can, or a nice early bed so as not to fear that early alarm. Think of it as one of those early flights for a holiday. Horrible but rewarding.

● ●

MAY 1ST

Give yourself a gentle pinch and punch for the first of the month. Happy 1st May to you. I wonder if you were able to get up and watch the sunset as instructed yesterday. If so . . .

Write a little poem or limerick about your experience. If not . . .

Sing, 'The sun has got his hat on, hip-hip-hip-hooray. The sun has got his hat on and he's coming out today' at least thrice, as a fun punishment. A funishment, if you will. Nice. It's a surprisingly fun song to put on to start the day.

MAY 2ND

Although we are working on improving our inner selves, and that's the most important and beautiful part of us, let's not forget we do live in a body we must love. It can help self-esteem to do something small to our outer appearance.

Have a nice PREEN. You could have a manicure or pedicure (ask a friend to do it if you can't get one professionally, or just massage your hands with some nice lotion). Do something to PREEN. (Good word – say it out loud to start the day – PREEN. Lovely.)

• •

MAY 3RD

More on the joy of words today. We have a language, we use words, let's have fun with them.

Play word cricket with colleagues in a meeting:

Choose a word that will be "your" word and every time some-one says it you get a point. E.g. I choose 'deliver', someone else chooses "project". Livens up an otherwise possibly dull meeting.

MAY 4TH

As you will have gathered by now, I regularly aim to persuade you into a group sing-a-long. It's not just an excellent and easy way to relax your nervous system but the connection with others reduces stress even more. Our instinct is often to isolate ourselves in tricky and anxious times, so fight against that if you can.

Do you remember singing rounds? At school? Get three or four of you (or more), sit in a round, and sing a round! Ideas for rounds: London's Burning. *Remember? Or* Frère Jacques.

● ●

MAY 5TH

Just to reverse some old sexist traditions . . .

Whistle at a builder and say he's got a nice arse!

MAY 6TH

Relationships are wonderful. Of course. But we can't deny they sometimes go wrong. Perhaps you have got involved with a person you know you shouldn't. Are you feeling scared to get out of a relationship? Or are you recovering from a break-up?

Put on I will Survive *by Gloria Gaynor – find the lyrics, too – and sing it like you mean it. Empower yourself. Because even if you feel alone at the moment, YOU WILL SURVIVE. And being single does not mean a lesser time in your life.*

NOTE: One joy of the single life – double bed to yourself EVERY night. STARFISH sleeping position here you come. Enjoy.

● ●

MAY 7TH

Are you feeling a bit irritated with your partner? Living with people isn't always easy. Don't bottle it all up.

Have a pillow fight! Who says they are just for kids or old-fashioned movies? NOT ME! Give him or her a gentle whack to get an irritation out and I guarantee you'll end up laughing. PILLOW FIGHT!

MAY 8TH

I am all about healthy eating. Absolutely. But of course, never to the exclusion of treating yourself from time to time. Perhaps once or twice a week nominate a day for a treat time. Today treat yourself with a massive dollop of Such Fun.

Buy a packet of your favourite biscuits. Crush them up with a rolling pin or masher. Get a hairdryer. Place the hairdryer one side of the biscuits and your mouth on the other side. Start the hairdryer and you will be playing BISCUIT BLIZZARD!

● ●

MAY 9TH

A random way to ring the changes today . . . Spontaneous ideas are often the best way to distract joyfully from those life worries.

Today I declare as MEXICAN DAY! Ideally find and wear a sombrero all day. If that's tricky say, 'Hola' as much as possible. If someone asks you a question, answer them, '¿Que?' Have some guacamole and corn chips. Have a burrito. Have a happy, for no reason, MEXICAN DAY – YAY!

MAY 10TH

Yesterday we had a fun day for ourselves thinking of another country. Now let's think outwards, knowing that being generous despite personal difficulties is a powerful message to ourselves and others.

Choose a country in the world that is suffering. Donate to a relevant charity if you can. Say a prayer. Light a candle. Do something for those worse off. And say three things you are incredibly grateful for about your own country.

● ●

MAY 11TH

Bird noise is often played in spas for relaxation. It is known as a sound that naturally makes humans feel safe and secure and therefore calmer. If there is bird song, there is no threat around. And nothing beats the real thing.

Find 10 minutes today to still your mind by focusing on and listening to bird song. Try and mimic it, see if they answer back! Have a little chat to the birds. A chance to have a stress-busting mindful moment in an otherwise busy day.

MAY 12TH

Remember we are doing daily Doses O' Fun for very good reason. Breaking old patterns, spreading joy, telling our minds and bodies we no longer want to be depressed or anxious.

I dare you to start a Mexican Wave! Could you do it on a bus, a train, outside in a traffic jam, in the office? Or, if not, just do one on your own. Up and down a few times you go – bit of exercise, if nothing else!

● ●

MAY 13TH

Are you a good listener? It's an amazing gift to be able to make people feel truly listened to. Here's a fun way to learn to listen.

Listen really intently to everyone today. Listen out for inadvertent song lyrics. And if you hear them, quickly sing the next line of the song! Someone's got to say something like, 'It's not unusual' (. . . to be loved by anyone – Tom Jones) or 'I tell you what I want' (. . . what I really, really want – Spice Girls). Happy Listening!

MAY 14TH

Following on from being a good listener yesterday, here's a more serious note on the same subject today.

When someone is talking to you, do NOT continue typing, texting or any kind of multi-tasking. Fix your eyes on to theirs and give them the time they need to chat.

'To be listened to is to be loved.' Alice Goodwin-Hudson

'If we can share our story with someone who responds with empathy and understanding, shame can't survive.' Brené Brown

● ●

MAY 15TH

Are you feeling bored with your job? In an ideal world we would all love our work but sometimes it can take a while to find the right thing. And even in the right job, there might be aspects to it that we find monotonous. Here follows an intricate idea to jolly up your working day.

PRETEND TO BE A SPY. Everything you do today, imagine you are a spy. Walking along the street to the office, follow someone. Or imagine you are being followed. When someone says to you, 'The office meeting is at three,' or whatever, reply, 'Roger, ten–four.' Sit down on a park bench next to someone. Imagine they are leaving you a package. Or I dare you to say, "The field is ready to be harvested" to someone and move off, as if you have given an order. If someone asks your name today, say surname first, then first name, à la James Bond. Do anything you like to FEEL LIKE A SPY.

MAY 16TH

Did you ever brave the 'going commando day' suggestion earlier in the year? If so, here's a chance to ramp it up a notch.

Wear just pants underneath a coat. Ideally, if you are going to pick up your beloved from a station or airport or somewhere, you can greet them with a, 'I have nothing on under here.' SAUCY.

NOTE: Be aware that if you go through security at the airport, you need an emergency plan if they want you to take off your coat!

• •

MAY 17TH

Encouraging people is such a kind thing to do. Everyone needs encouraging. We can get so caught up in our own stuff we forget there might be others feeling equally low about themselves.

Think of some family members or friends you haven't seen for a while. Perhaps some godchildren, nieces or nephews? Send them a postcard with some encouraging words.

I MEAN, AREN'T YOU LOVELY?!

MAY 18TH

Talking about being lovely . . .

Today, let someone go in front of you in a shopping queue.

Or, if are feeling it and are able to be incredibly generous, pay for the person in front of you. (Always important to make sure they don't have a concealed trolley full of a vast amount of shopping before you offer!)

I will say it again: AREN'T YOU LOVELY?! Say, 'Yes, Miranda.' Thank you.

● ●

MAY 19TH

For being so lovely, let's think about treating ourselves. If there is one meal I believe should make a big formal come-back it's AFTERNOON TEA.

Plan to have an afternoon tea. Teapots full of your tea of choice, crustless sandwiches (egg, salmon, cucumber), small cakes but the key and if nothing else . . . SCONES, CREAM AND JAM. Such a treat.

NOTE: I put the cream on first, as in my head it's the butter equivalent. But apparently the rule in polite society is jam first. WHO CARES?!

MAY 20TH

I do not endorse anything that causes a public disturbance. But in the name of jollity I wonder whether this is allowed . . .

Put some bath bombs or fairy liquid in a public fountain. Play in the BUBBLES!

NAUGHTY MIRANDA!

NOTE: If you think this is irresponsible (the jury is out) then enjoy a bath with a bath bomb.

• •

MAY 21ST

Do you want to feel REALLY organised and your To Do list is not inspiring you right now?

It's May but, hey, go and buy a couple of Christmas presents for a few loved ones. Wrap them up, put them away. HOW ORGANISED ARE YOU? Celebrate with an eggnog! Or an unseasonal snack of choice. Can you find a mince pie in May?

MAY 22ND

I don't know about you but I have always wanted to see a flash mob for real – even YouTube clips of them cheer me up.

Why don't you do a mini flash mob?! Learn a short routine with some friends at home and then choose a time and a location – shop, park, the school gates, wherever – and burst into the routine. BRILLIANT.

• •

MAY 23RD

I regularly suggest lots of fun around dancing and songs – it's amazing how freeing they are. Today is on a similar theme but slightly different.

Act like a professional dancer! Do a stretch at the bus stop, as if you were at the Royal Ballet. Do some random jazz hands. Say 'Five, six, seven and eight' at least 3 times. Stand in first and second ballet position regularly. Walk with the elegance and poise of a dancer. Wear Lycra if you are brave enough. Have a day imagining you are a dancer!

MAY 24TH

Want to spice up your morning routine? The morning is a great time to break habits before those anxious thoughts creep in.

Let someone else in the household choose what you are going to wear today. You HAVE to wear what they suggest! If there is a child under 7 in the house, let them choose it – more risky but more FUN.

••••••••••••••••••••••••••••••

MAY 25TH

Sometimes I find myself suffering from nostalgia and yearning for the freedom of childhood. It is usually a sign that I am getting swamped by the responsibilities of being an adult and need to step away for a moment.

Re-read your favourite children's book. Escape again. Remember how it felt to be so excited about the world you were reading. WONDERFUL.

NOTE: If you don't have access to any children's books then how about a lovely children's film? *Nanny McPhee* anyone? *The Railway Children*?

MAY 26TH

Did you ever read *The Wind in the Willows*? I love and agree with the quote by Ratty: 'Believe me, my young friend, there is nothing — absolutely nothing — half so much worth doing as simply messing about in boats.'

Today, if you can, MESS ABOUT IN A BOAT! Hire a rowing boat. Or a pedalo. Go on a river cruise. Or try a CANOE! Happy boat messing.

NOTE: Perhaps this is something you can plan to do with the kids at half term. Not that you ever need children as an excuse to have such fun according to the rules of *Miranda's Daily Dose of Such Fun*.

● ●

MAY 27TH

If adults had some of the spontaneous in-the-moment freedom of children, they could only be but happier.

Whether you have children or not, have a go on the local swings or slide. I once got stuck in a children's slide. I decided it wasn't embarrassing and styled it out good and proper. Lay there and had a little snooze!

MAY 28TH

Everyone needs a moment to feel glamorous, a chance to tell themselves they are handsome and/or beautiful. Basically, we all want to occasionally feel like James Bond or a Bond Girl, don't we?

Get dressed up and have a cocktail. Ideally at a bar. Choose a mocktail if you don't drink. Drink in the atmosphere and then, indeed, drink in the drink. Such fun.

NOTE: This could be a date night idea if you want to get some romance back in your relationship. And you can always do this at home, if a bar isn't an option. Maybe get dressed up and surprise your partner with your look when they get home and present them with a cocktail. Aaaaaah!

• •

MAY 29TH

I realize I miss so much of life by looking at my phone when getting from A to B. I can't remember what it was like when I was younger walking about without one, which saddens me. We are missing so much. Here's a fun way to make you more mindful of life around you.

Look out for planes and birds today. When you see one point and say, 'Is it a bird, is it a plane, is it Superman? Nope, it's just a bird,' or, 'It's just a plane,' if it's a plane. You'll have fun seeing how many people look up wondering what amazing thing you might be looking at! And you'll have to put your phone away to do it.

MAY 30TH

Meal times with family and friends can be rushed or, dare I say it, they may have become conversationally dull.

Play Three Lies, One Truth. Make 3 statements, only 1 of which is true, and let people guess which the true one is. A chance to startle the family. Or do 5 quick-fire quiz questions for everyone. Try and find out some interesting details about your friends or family that you never knew before.

●●●●●●●●●●●●●●●●●●●●●●●●●●●●

MAY 31ST

Right. Concentrate. This Daily Dose of Such Fun for you and others is a little more complicated than normal.

1. With the friends and/or family you chose to play with, work out a funny motionless pose.

2. Walk around a public place (street, shop etc.) and one of you says, 'Assume the position.'

3. When this is stated, then you must all assume your previously decided pose. Stay still for a few moments, then walk on as if nothing unusual happened. You can do this as much as you like – when someone says, 'Assume the position' you simply must!

This idea was given to me by The Meldrum Family in Sussex, who regularly 'Assume the position', if you pardon.

JUNE

. . . .

JUNE 1ST

I have decided that today, because it's a new month, is PRIZE DAY! We all deserve to be rewarded for just being ourselves, accomplishments aside.

Make some prizes. Get some labels or Post-It notes and write things like, "Best person of the day", "Best hair of the day" or "Gold prize for brilliance today". And then go around handing them out to friends and strangers. It's Prize Day. People need to be awarded your unique prizes!

JUNE 2ND

In case you hadn't gathered, I LOVE animals. They make me smile. And they are excellent stress busters and known for reducing blood pressure. In an ideal world I would be constantly surrounded by small fluffy creatures.

Go to a pet shop or a local animal centre. Stroke the bunnies. Commune with a lesser-known animal. Touch a turtle. Maybe even buy a fish.

NOTE: If you can't get to the real deal then spend half an hour looking at cute YouTube animal clips. SO cheering and funny.

• •

JUNE 3RD

Today let's do something to surprise others and give them something new to think about. You might just stop someone from having a panic attack with this distraction (and hopefully not cause one!).

Go into a kitchen or hardware shop. Set all the egg timers or clocks to go off at the same time. The more egg timers the better. When they go off, do a celebratory dance and round of applause and run out shouting, 'Such fun, such fun!'

NOTE: You can also do this at home to surprise your family.

JUNE 4TH

Today is about getting in touch with our bodies. Very unBritish, Miranda, I hear you say. But our bodies are what take us through life and we often ignore them until they get ill. It's vital to check in with how they are feeling – they often tell us we are stressed before we know it.

Say thank you to each part of your body. 'Thank you feet for walking me around.' 'Thank you fingers for allowing me to feel, and eat.' 'Thank you eyes for letting me see.' 'Thank you legs for allowing me to gallop.' Keep thanking your body. Get in touch with your body. Check it out for any aches and pains that might need attendance.

NOTE: You can also tell other people they have fabulous bodies. In a non-sexual way, please! I am not encouraging you to be lewd.

● ●

JUNE 5TH

Following on from the body theme yesterday, here's an idea to feel really present and connected with your body.

Go skinny dipping. SO FREEING. If it's not possible for you to do it today, then plan a skinny dip – to a lake, or a private pool, if you are going on holiday soon. Plan to dip in the NUDE. Cheeky!

JUNE 6TH

If the idea of a skinny dip yesterday felt too much and you want to do something else nourishing and soothing for your body, then today's the day for you.

Have a really indulgent bath. With BUBBLES. Have a bubble bath. Make a bubble beard. A bubble hat. A bubble pair of long johns. Soak your body in bubbles. Maybe put on some Michael BUBLÉ to listen to.

● ●

JUNE 7TH

Today is about remembering to acknowledge and respect others, as well as our usual dose of fun kindness. It's easy to judge people and not respect their life decisions. But ultimately it never makes us feel good.

Everyone you meet or interact with today – bow or curtsey.

NOTE: Be careful if you curtsey because, as you rise up, it can cause a release of bottom wind.

JUNE 8TH

Women need to be told they are beautiful; it's an innate need.

Go up to at least one woman you know today, kiss their hand and theatrically but truthfully say, 'My dear you are ravishingly beautiful.' And indeed feel beautiful yourself for doing such a lovely thing.

NOTE: You could also risk doing this to a complete stranger. A beautiful friendship might ensue.

●●●●●●●●●●●●●●●●●●●●●●●●●●●●●●

JUNE 9TH

Summer is hopefully very much in the air by now. The days are longer. Problems seem less intense, I find, in the summer. But if you are feeling wound up, the summer gives us lovely ways to relax.

Make a daisy chain. Wear it on your head. Channel a relaxed hippie vibe. Enjoy the feel and look of the lovely daisies as you make your chain.

JUNE 10TH

I have a number of favourite words. But they are often hard to get into one short sentence. But I have found a way with three favourite words: quiche, portion and moist.

See if you can order a MOIST PORTION OF QUICHE. Such fun.

NOTE: Really relish saying and articulating the words as you order. Also, perhaps ask for some relish. That's another good word. Please to relish the word relish.

● ●

JUNE 11TH

Welcome to Miranda's Medieval Day! Random – I know, that's the point. It's going to drive out those fearful and habitual thoughts, and give you another clear focus. Hopefully you are learning you can switch yourself out of difficult moods by ignoring those pesky thoughts and focusing on my Daily Doses of Fun.

GO MEDIEVAL. It might be tricky for women to wear a full medieval dress or men to go about with a sword (but I would like someone to try the latter!), so go medieval with your language.

Use the following words: 'Anon' instead of 'Bye/laters'; 'Good morrow' instead of 'Good morning'; and 'Prithee' instead of 'Please'. Call everyone 'Sire'. You could also try and get 'hither' and 'thither' into your medieval parlance today.

JUNE 12TH

A silly dare to free you up physically and mentally.

Walk around your block, or go somewhere further if you dare, with a pair of knickers, ideally a coloured thong, OVER YOUR TROUSERS.

Style it out good and proper.

● ●

JUNE 13TH

You may be on a diet, or being careful about your eating (and if so, WELL DONE), but it's the summer and you are allowed at least one ice cream during it.

Go and buy yourself a Cornetto. But ask for it by singing, 'Just one Cornetto, give it to me.' Obviously. How anyone can buy one without doing that is frankly confusing.

JUNE 14TH

Feeling grounded and centred is great for calming your nervous system. An easy way to do this is by focusing on feeling the ground beneath you.

Walk barefoot on some grass. Perhaps you could also sing The Bare Necessities *from* The Jungle Book *at the same time? And do a few little dance moves. Feel that grass. LOVELY!*

NOTE: Don't you love the smell of cut grass in the summer, too? Have a sniff if there is any about!

● ●

JUNE 15TH

Although in recent years I have tried to cook every night, and be as organic as possible for physical and mental well-being, sometimes it's just not possible, we are too busy. A microwaveable meal beckons.

Sing my ready meal celebratory song loudly in the shop (the tune is up to you):

'Praise M&S (insert supermarket you are in) for putting food on the table,

'Coz cooking drives us crazy,

'We're busy slash lazy,

'Other supermarket chains are available.'

JUNE 16TH

As you probably know, the Romans were known for eating lying down. How wonderfully grand and decadent!

Have a toga evening! Fashion them out of sheets and towels and lie about eating grapes and finger food like a Roman. Be decadent!

NOTE: As you enjoy your decadence, remember you deserve to be kind to yourself. You are doing fabulously. Don't listen to any of those mean thoughts towards yourself. They are nasty little lies we all have. I now view them no differently to a headache. Annonying, but not going to ruin my life.

● ●

JUNE 17TH

Food is not only an essential need for the body, but it can be fab mind and soul nourishment. We are so lucky to have access to good food.

Give a delicious sandwich to someone in need. And really savour every taste you experience today.

JUNE 18TH

I am not a fan of clothes shopping. I get bored and hot and claustrophobic! And I find taking my clothes on and off EXHAUSTING. But it is, of course, often an essential expedition. So here's something to jolly up a clothes shopping trip.

I dare you to have a full-blown imaginary conversation with a mannequin. At one point laugh and say, 'Oh, you are funny' to confuse people into thinking you really are conversing or, indeed, that the mannequin is real.

● ●

JUNE 19TH

As the saying goes, 'Laughter is the best medicine.' Well, it is, indeed, proven to release happy hormones. Often adults get stuck in a rut of not laughing for days. Time to unlock this.

Play some old children's games. Heads, shoulders, knees and toes anyone? The chocolate game? Remember that?! Chinese whispers?

JUNE 20TH

Yesterday I mentioned Chinese whispers. If this book is about freeing ourselves up and spreading joy, I dare someone to . . .

Start a game of Chinese whispers in a public place. Bus? Tube? School dining room?

It may be too tricky but I'd love to hear if someone manages it!

● ●

JUNE 21ST

Welcome to the longest day of the year. Say, 'Hello, Long Day, how very lovely and long you are.' Take a deep breath, summer is really here and there are good times ahead.

Have a long day. Wear a long skirt or shirt. Potter on your tiptoes to feel longer. If you are naturally long, claim this is YOUR day – show off about reaching all those high shelves. Have a drink in a long glass. Eat some long food – spaghetti? Have a long bath. Make a long phone call. Happy LONG day.

JUNE 22ND

Are you accepting yet that you are SENSATIONAL? Truly, you are. And, frankly, what's the point in NOT believing that. You are stuck with you, for life. Love yourself.

Go to a chemist and say, 'Do you have anything that could help me? I have a problem. I am SENSATIONAL! Don't worry, I think it's probably incurable, bye!' If that's too shy-making for you, then at least once today when someone asks how you are answer with, 'I AM SENSATIONAL.'

● ●

JUNE 23RD

We might be British, but we are allowed to be sexy! Are you lacking the nerve to feel like a sexual person?

Wear some leggings or stretchy trousers, put a cushion down the back, put on Beyoncé's Crazy in Love *and dance as if you have the best butt in the world. Really work that bottom. I want some hip thrusts, some twerking, do it all! Be Beyoncé!*

JUNE 24TH

Working in an office in the summer during nice weather can be tough, as we yearn to be outside on a beautiful day. But, as you know, I like to find ways to jolly up office life.

I challenge you to LAMINATE A SLICE OF HAM OR CHEESE!

NOTE: If this breaks the laminator please neither blame nor invoice me.

• •

JUNE 25TH

Happy 25th June to you! It's six months to Christmas.

It's the summer, but have a carol singing day. Ding and dong merrily on high in JUNE. Crazy Such Fun times.

JUNE 26TH

Always look on the bright side of life. A great song. A good way to live. But often very hard to put into practice. This might help.

Have a BRIGHT YELLOW DAY. Welcome to Yellow Day. Wear yellow, eat yellow, answer questions with yellow, where possible. You can always turn yellow into a glorious extended 'y–helloooo–w' to everyone.

• •

JUNE 27TH

Adult colouring books became the rage because it was a chance for us to just be in the moment, like children.

So, wait for it, DO SOME COLOURING! If you are a very neat and tidy person, do something chaotic/messy/abstract. And if you are a messy person, try something very neat and within the lines.

"If you hear a voice within you say, 'You cannot paint,' then, by all means, paint and that voice will be silenced." Vincent Van Gogh

JUNE 28TH

Traffic needn't be stressful. No, really, it needn't. What can we do about it, anyway? It's better for mind, body and soul to sit there peacefully rather than rage against it.

Turn to someone at the traffic lights and mouth 'I love you'. See what happens!

NOTE: If you end up getting married to the person you did this to then, please, can I come to the wedding? Thanks.

● ●

JUNE 29TH

Some people doing jobs in authority get a hard time. Remember they are just people, like you, doing a job. Often we forget the human behind the uniform.

Go up to someone in authority – the bank manager, a police-man – and say, 'Hello, you are doing a great job. Have a nice day.' Or give a traffic warden a "ticket" in the form of a badge, label or note saying, 'I am marvellous.' Traffic wardens need some love too.

JUNE 30TH

Want a spring in your step today?

Walk with a spring in your step. LITERALLY! Simple.

● ●

JULY

• •

JULY 1ST

I not only love a musical but I do think life would be better if it was all a bit musical theatre. Jolly, camp and vibrant. So let's welcome in the first of July by going Musical Camp today.

Do a daily chore in the style of a musical. Suggestion: unload the dishwasher with a friend or partner. Sing to them, 'Darling, please put this plate away!' Their reply, 'Certainly, my love.' Ceremoniously remove each item dancing around the kitchen as much like a West End musical performer as possible! I want to see jazz hands with those mugs and jugs (ooh, steady).

JULY 2ND

I remember when I was feeling particularly down, a friend bought me bottles of bubbles – you know, the ones we used to play with as kids. I was sceptical, but actually it really helped change my state of mind.

GET BLOWING BUBBLES! Look at the light reflecting on them, the magic when they pop. See how big you can make a bubble. Try doing it outside and see them blow in the wind before they pop. Or run after them and pop them. The joyful inner child can but appear when there are beautiful bubbles in the air!

NOTE: You can make bubble mixture with washing-up liquid and water, if you can't buy any. Oh, and if you have a dog they can go mad trying to pop them – funny.

● ●

JULY 3RD

Today, let's reduce those bad sugars and instead think FRUIT. (Sugar is not our mind or body's friend – sorry if this is news to you. It's just for special treats.)

Buy some weird, unusual fruits. Try one you have never had before. Kumquat anyone? Choose anything. But I do like to say 'Kumquat'. Repeat after me: KUMQUAT. Have fun with your funny fruit.

JULY 4TH

I know we aren't always good at chitchat with strangers, but have you noticed when a nice spontaneous chat does happen it's rather cheering? Helps you feel more connected and positive, even if you think it's the last thing you need.

If someone asks, 'Do you have the time?' say, 'I do, indeed, my good fellow. Aren't you lovely? It's what I call [INSERT TIME]. Although, that will change – ha, ha.'

If no one asks you the time, ask someone the time and then say, 'Thank you, you are lovely and I wish you on your merry way for a merry day.'

● ●

JULY 5TH

I sometimes find the summer hard when I feel down. It feels like there is an expectation to be happy. And feeling down when the sun is out sucks. But don't worry, I have plenty of fun ideas to help. Simple summer fun today.

Find a grassy verge or hill and roll down it. Lie horizontally to it and push yourself off. Weeeeeeeee!

JULY 6TH

Are you ready for a dare? I am daring you today, big time. It will really make you and others laugh. Are you ready, this is a PROPER dare. Drum role please. . . .

Drive around the block – TOPLESS! (I will still be proud if you go in a bra, or bra on top of your clothes)

NOTE: I have done the topless dare once. I have never laughed so much at traffic lights, hoping against hope that someone would look over! They did. Not a flattering reaction but a very funny one.

• •

JULY 7TH

Pottering is SO good for you. Not jogging, not power walking, not being in a rush, just pottering, as if you were a very old Italian lady in the heat. Changing your pace sends positive, relaxing messages to your mind.

Potter today. Be it to the station, school, bus . . . Or get off a stop early. Look around as you potter, too – what do you notice? The sky, the noises, the people. And put your phone AWAY! Get pottering.

JULY 8TH

Rest is an essential part of life. Find moments to be still.
Reduce all that rushing about. We all do it – when I rush I feel
like an oversized meerkat (there's an image for you).

*Lie in the sun – or on a comfy sofa, or even on your bed – for
10 minutes. Pretend you are on holiday. Breathe deeply. Listen
to two of your favourite songs. Take time in the stillness to
really savour them.*

Song suggestions: *Holiday* by Madonna (obviously); *Walking
on Sunshine*; *Copacabana*; *Loco in Acapulco*.

● ●

JULY 9TH

Oh how I continue to struggle with mornings, even in the
summer. Apparently the first 7 minutes of the day sets your
mood for the day. Bit challenging!

*This morning, when you brush your hair, brush it UP instead of
DOWN. See what happens. Present your new style to your loved
ones at breakfast. Or take a selfie and post it to some people
for morning laughs.*

Thank you, Bella, for this idea. Bella, my dear friend who this
book is dedicated to, died way too early, like many people we
know. She would love to think of you all appreciating your life
and smiling as you brush your hair up!

JULY 10TH

The summer months are the best time to explore the beauty of nature. And being in nature really helps to soothe stressed nervous systems.

Make a wand out of a stick and walk around all day magicking everything beautiful with a flamboyant wave of your wand. As if it were you who created the beautiful things you see. Basically become a camp fairy godmother for a fun way to be really mindful of the beauty you may otherwise miss. If this is too much for the introverts, pick four beautiful things today to appreciate.

NOTE: I sometimes find studying the intricacies of a flower makes me feel connected to the universe. My problems feel somehow shared, less important, and, if nothing else, focusing on such beauty gives your mind a rest from those whirring thoughts.

● ●

JULY 11TH

Mindfulness was one of the greatest tools I had for maintaining a calmer mind when I had recovered from anxiety. When I discovered it, I realized quite how stressed I was and how much of life I missed. What a waste of time!

If you can afford it, buy Mindfulness: a Practical Guide to Finding Peace in a Frantic World *by Mark Williams and Dr Danny Penman.*

JULY 12TH

A well-known mindfulness exercise is to buy some seeds, plant them and watch them grow over time. It keeps you in the moment, moves you out of busy doing mode to just being. So you may guess today's idea.

BUY AND PLANT SOME SEEDS!

NOTE: Look ahead to tomorrow's idea, in case you want to prepare for that, too, whilst you are buying seeds.

● ●

JULY 13TH

Have you heard of Guerrilla Gardening? Planting for the community.

Get some bulbs or some already-flowering small plants, like pansies, and plant them under a tree on your street or some-where in the neighbourhood. Fun to do and gives everyone around you some beauty. Also, when you walk past them you can say, 'Wow, I wonder what wonderfully amazing creative generous person did that for our neighbourhood!'

"It's the simple things in life that are the most extraordinary."
Paulo Coelho

JULY 14TH

Here's a fun fact for you – I am about a 32nd Native American Indian. Yes, really! Call me Pocahontas.

Be a NATIVE AMERICAN INDIAN! Make a wigwam. (Bamboo sticks/long sticks held together by string for the framework, a rug pegged on with clothes pegs and – boom – wigwam.) Put some feathers in your hair. Make up a personal American Indian dance to do outside your wigwam. Have a picnic in your wigwam. WIGWAM AWAY!

• •

JULY 15TH

Now, where do you stand on camping? Some people love it; others need their luxury. If you are the former, rekindle your love for it; get back in touch with your childhood passion. If you are the latter, step out of your comfort zone and be more grateful for your bed when you get back to it.

HI-DE-HI CAMPERS! The challenge is to go camping. Spend the night in a tent. It can just be in the back garden, if you want. Look at the stars, get in touch with night-time, with no electricity, and tell stories. Maybe even get a fire going and toast some marshmallows or sausages on a stick. FUN, FUN.

JULY 16TH

Yesterday I suggested camping. Today something silly on a theme for larks.

BE CAMP! Have a stereotypically camp day. Call people 'Duckie' and 'Darling'. Walk with a camp gait. Wear pink, especially if you are male. Dance to I'm Coming Out. *Go celebratory GAY. YAY!*

● ●

JULY 17TH

Why don't you break some family routines that might have found you in a rut and cause some fun chaos. Let off some steam.

Get some balloons. Fill them with water. Put them in a bowl. Get the family outside. Chuck water bombs at them. A crazy game of chase will ensue.

JULY 18TH

More simple summer jollity. And because it's one of my favourite things to do.

HAVE A PICNIC! Choose a spot, get a rug and your favourite picnic foods. Scotch egg anyone? Yes, please. SUCH FUN. I LOVE a picnic.

NOTE: I want to hear from people who have picnics in lay-bys by or in their cars on busy roads because I need an explanation!

● ●

JULY 19TH

Welcome to Miranda's "For-no-reason-other-than-it-will-be-fun" HAWAIIAN DAY!

Do as much as you can today on a Hawaiian theme. Wear a grass skirt (or just a floaty skirt), buy some cheap garlands and hand them out – Hawaiian office day?! – but mainly do hula hula moves for no reason. You can always put on the Aloha Oe song for extra effect.

NOTE: Maybe organize a spontaneous Hawaiian party – text some mates forthwith.

JULY 20TH

Have you eaten lots of lovely fruit this month? Well done. Now it's treat time. As you treat yourself, don't forget to acknowledge that you are being kind to yourself. Stop judging yourself – all an essential part of anxiety management.

Treat yourself to a childhood favourite snack. Maybe you haven't had a packet of Discos for years. Do you want some naughty sweeties? Sit down, savour the taste of your youth and tell yourself you are worth treating.

• •

JULY 21ST

Children shouldn't get *all* the fun.

Are you anywhere near a kids' ball pool? If so, dive in and have a good roll around!

JULY 22ND

Anything I suggest for just a laugh is indeed just for laughs but, remember, doing these sometimes deeply random things habitually will help your brain re-route to think more positively.

Today do an impression of a chicken at least 3 times. (Yes, particularly random today.) You can do it as disguised or as full-on as you like. I am imagining at least one of you at the photocopier at work suddenly doing a cluck, cluck noise and ruffling some feathers!

● ●

JULY 23RD

As a child of the '80s, I can't help but love a music video with a wind machine.

If you have a large fan (and it might even be worth finding or buying one for the joy of this) then put on an '80's classic of your choice. Stand in front of it and assume classic pop star poses. Feel sexy. Let your hair sway behind you. Have a full-on pop goddess moment. Very empowering.

NOTE: Sticking your head out of a car window (if safe) can be an alternative, if you are not with fan.

JULY 24TH

I don't think we compliment each other enough. A compliment goes a long way to help people feel better about themselves. Focus your compliments on their personality, not just their outer appearance. People like to feel really known for who they are.

TELL SOMEONE TODAY THEY ARE FABULOUS, AND GIVE A SPECIFIC REASON WHY.

NOTE: If you receive a compliment today, remember to accept it gratefully and not bat it away like a typical Brit!

• •

JULY 25TH

On the compliment theme from yesterday, I think we mostly compliment women, don't we?

Compliment a man today. Tell him he looks very handsome, courageous, charming, has nice hair or whatever it might be. Men – brave it – compliment your fellow man. We all know you're rubbish at that!

JULY 26TH

Summer is the season to feel more free generally. To celebrate that we must do our seasonal SUMMER GALLOP.

Gallop in a public place! As it's the summer, perhaps find a park, field, or green area of some kind and sing the Black Beauty *theme. Channel your inner horse. A neigh or two would be a lovely addition for the Summer Gallop!*

●●●●●●●●●●●●●●●●●●●●●●●●●●●●●

JULY 27TH

Talking of channelling your inner horse, here's a very silly idea for today. And one that I am unashamedly happy to admit I do regularly.

At 3 points in the day imagine yourself as a dressage horse! Do a few proud, neat-footed manoeuvres. A gentle trot. A proud prance. Dressage away. Use your arms and hands as your 3rd and 4th legs!

JULY 28TH

It is always hard to accept the phrase 'Money doesn't make you happy' when money is tight. But there are studies that show those that win the lottery or make a lot of money in business go back to their baseline of happiness within a year or two. So, if they weren't happy before, they stay unhappy.

Give away what money you can today. Donate to a charity close to your heart, or give something to a friend or stranger in need. As you do it, feel happy you aren't stuck in the belief that the more money you have, the happier you will be.

'To be upset over what you don't have is to waste what you do have.' Ken S. Keyes

● ●

JULY 29TH

It is possible to get our baseline of happiness up. To rewire ourselves to a more positive place. That's worth working towards. Here is another Daily Dose of Such Fun to help us on our way to that.

At home, or in your workplace, or in the park with friends – START A CONGA! See how many people you can get to join in. Who's got the longest conga? (As ever, not a euphemism.)

JULY 30TH

This might amuse you and others around you – I am imagining it happening in a shopping mall to cheer up those having to work and shop inside on a summer's day.

Go down an escalator doing a parody of Titanic. *Stand behind a friend, stretch out your arms and shout 'I'm King of the World' as you descend. And, of course, you could always throw in the Celine Dion song for good measure.*

• •

JULY 31ST

Yesterday it was Such Fun larks with an escalator. Today . . .

Have a showbiz moment on some stairs! As you descend a stair-case, do a high leg kick – really make a showbiz entrance. Finish with a fantastic pose!

NOTE: As you pose, feel the strength and confidence it gives you. Say to yourself, 'I am a good and attractive person.' BECAUSE YOU ARE. Remember, strong powerful poses with your body send positive messages to your brain.

AUGUST

• •

AUGUST 1ST

G'day, mate and welcome to August. Today's the day for a barbie. Get that rusty old BBQ out. Rain or shine. Or buy one of those cheap makeshift ones.

Today is all about putting your favourite bit of meat between two baps. WHY IS EVERYTHING A EUPHEMISM?! Grill that meat, lather on the ketchup and mustard and sink into a summer bap. YUM.

AUGUST 2ND

Sometimes it's good to remind yourself that, however important you are in this world (and you really are), your worries can feel way bigger than they actually are. Let's get some perspective.

Lie under the stars tonight. Realize you are a connected part of a massive universe. Have a star-based sing-a-long. Lucy in the Sky with Diamonds? Twinkle, Twinkle? *As you look at the stars remember that, just by being you, YOU ARE A STAR. It's time to think about shining brightly in the world.*

● ●

AUGUST 3RD

Do you need to free yourself up a bit at the moment? Feeling the need to be a bit daring? Want to feel more courageous?

Walk around naked! I am NOT suggesting in a supermarket . . . Just at home, if you haven't been naked for a while. Or you could be really daring and run naked in the garden or have a nude sunbathe.

NOTE: I once walked into a rehearsal room stark naked and stood at the door as if it was perfectly normal. Cue hilarious reactions before I ran back to put my clothes on. But it made me feel braver about performing that night!

AUGUST 4TH

Why do we love getting flowers? Surely, amongst bringing beauty into our homes, it makes us feel loved and cherished.

Today pick or buy some flowers and GET SCATTERING! Place them on people's doorsteps. Hand them out to people in the street saying, 'You are more beautiful than this flower.' Give a bunch to a loved one (so romantic to get flowers for no reason other than love). SCATTER SUMMER LOVE VIA A FLOWER.

• •

AUGUST 5TH

It may be summer but are you struggling to relax? It's so important to take some time out every day to breathe deeply and relax your body. Did you know that just by sitting, closing your eyes and remembering in as much detail as possible a relaxing time or an image you love, you can relax the body? Do that today if you are unable to do today's task.

Lie in a hammock for at least 10 minutes. Swing, sway, sink into it. SO RELAXING.

AUGUST 6TH

If you are lucky enough to have a garden, perk it up with a new purchase. Remind yourself that spending time outside in nature is calming for the soul.

Go on a trip to a GARDEN CENTRE. Buy something that relaxes or amuses you. A new garden recliner. If money is tight, buy some seeds and have a little sow today! Try a swing seat in the garden centre – have a rock in it. SUCH FUN.

NOTE: If you are a teenager and have never been to a garden centre, try it. Go on. You might find a mooning gnome. Oh, they exist! Talking of which, look ahead to tomorrow's entry if you do go to a garden centre today.

● ●

AUGUST 7TH

I mentioned gnomes yesterday. And now I can't quite let go of this idea.

Buy a gnome and place it secretly in the garden so that the family is wondering where on EARTH it came from. You could even write a letter, as if from the gnome, and tie it around the gnome (good word GNOME):-

'Hi. I am Gordon the Gnome and I would like to make this my home.'

AUGUST 8TH

Sometimes it's good to get messy. Let go of the inner control freak. Let the family cause a bit of mess in the kitchen and don't immediately clean it up.

Eat ice cream and jelly with chopsticks. CHAOS!

● ●

AUGUST 9TH

On the theme of control freak-ery, do you think you might be a perfectionist? Not able to let your standards drop? Do you believe that achievement leads to self-esteem?

Achieve NOTHING today. Just be. And every time you go to the bathroom, look in the mirror and say, 'I am a wonderful loved person just because I am me, not because of accomplishments.' If there are things you need to do, do them in a relaxed way and at a level that doesn't have to be "perfect".

AUGUST 10TH

I am not a fan of detoxes but it's good for mind and body to have a day of eating a little less.

Eat with your fingers today. Lite bites. It's NON-CUTLERY DAY!

NOTE: It's slightly cheating if you are free enough to eat a pie or fish and chips in public with just your hands. This is the only day I would say to wonderful people like you, curtail your freedom!

• •

AUGUST 11TH

Have you got some fruit in the bowl you know is going to go off before you eat it? (NAUGHTY, but we've all been there.)

Make some Fruit Friends! Or if you don't feel in the mood, pop all that fruit into your whizzer and – boom – you have a summer smoothie.

AUGUST 12TH

This is a very simple thing I adore to do in the summer.

Lie under a tree and look up at the sky in between the leaves.
Look at the wonderful patterns on the leaves. See some of the
patterns of the sun fall on you through the branches. SO
RELAXING. And imagine yourself as strong as that tree. If any
nasty thoughts come to mind, just see them as a breeze through
the branches, but the tree remains strong.

If you find it hard to be with your thoughts and need to be
doing something then pick a leaf and draw it. Or do one of
those leaf rubbings. (Put the leaf under the paper and draw
over it with a pencil.)

● ●

AUGUST 13TH

Did you know that what you say has an influential effect on
your well-being? Your words are a powerful weapon.

Whenever someone asks you how you are, answer with, 'It's
summertime, and the living is easy.' Sing it once. Maybe by
saying life is easy it will start to help make you feel better. And
if you are feeling great, this will be a fun day.

NOTE: Put the song on when you get home tonight. It's pretty
amazing.

AUGUST 14TH

Do you like sushi? It's very good for you, you know. Go and treat yourself but have fun blessing others whilst you do.

Go to a sushi restaurant with a conveyor belt. Write little notes, like 'You are beautiful' or 'You rock' on Post-Its and pop them next to the dishes. Then when fellow diners pick up a dish they get a lovely note too.

NOTE: If the restaurant manager looks cross, tell them Miranda said to do it!

● ●

AUGUST 15TH

Another way for adults to reclaim the joys of youth today.

BUILD A SANDCASTLE! If you aren't lucky enough to live near a beach, go to a children's playground where there is a sandpit. SUCH FUN.

AUGUST 16TH

To reduce any panicky sensations, remember to stay grounded, to help you feel safe and connected. An easy way of doing this is to consciously notice your feet on the floor. However, with today's Dollop O' Fun I'm suggesting the opposite. But hopefully it will make you aware of the concept of grounding even more. Clever? Well, I thought so!

Spend the day trying to avoid touching the ground as much as possible! Hop on the odd bench you walk past. Travel down the office on a wheelie chair. Scramble over furniture at home. Spend moments 'in the air'!

● ●

AUGUST 17TH

I love the fresh air. Which is one reason I don't like gyms. (I will keep on saying it – THEY SMELL OF CROTCH.) A good breath of fresh air can be so invigorating. But then there's the issue of THE RAIN. But today (or when it next rains) don't let that stop you.

DANCE IN THE RAIN. Don't care how wet you get. Feel the fresh rain on your face. Feel FREE as you dance in the rain!

NOTE: Enjoy styling out the wet shirt issue. Always awkward.

AUGUST 18TH

It can be very hard for us all not to get bogged down in our own overwhelming emotions so today there is another unique distraction to think beyond them.

Get a prize (can be anything you want – a box of chocolates, maybe) and spend the day going up to strangers and asking if you can guess their name. Give the prize away if you happen to guess right. Imagine that – it would be quite the celebration! If you don't guess a name, then give the prize to a stranger anyway.

● ●

AUGUST 19TH

Are you getting bored with your food choices? Need another way to make some different kinds of meals?

Ask a child to give you a menu of what to eat today. Eat EXACTLY that!

GOOD LUCK!

AUGUST 20TH

Last month I suggested having a star gaze to put your earthly worries into perspective. Today . . .

SAVOUR THE MOON! Have a moon-watching moment. Put the song The Whole of the Moon *on. Do a moon dance. You could even moon a member of your family! Happy Mooning.*

● ●

AUGUST 21ST

When I feel tired and down I find it very hard to get myself to exercise, even though I know it will help, not only in that moment, but also for stress and general health as a whole. This might help you if you ever feel the same. I often do it.

Get a stopwatch (there should be one on your phone) and for 20 minutes do a different movement each minute. Jog on the spot, then skip, then do a dance move, then some punching . . . whatever it might be. Make it up. But change it every minute. The 20 minutes will fly by and you will have done a lovely bit of exercise that was actually fun. FUNERCISE. Thank you.

AUGUST 22ND

I have childhood memories of running through sprinklers in the summer.

Run through a sprinkler! If you don't have one, use a hose – hose down your friends. Or, if you dare, go to one of those public fountains that spray up from the ground. Stand over it and wait to be sprinkled!

• •

AUGUST 23RD

Silly and simple today.

Have a STRIPY DAY! Wear something stripy. Eat something stripy (streaky bacon anyone?!). Have a look out for all things stripy. If you see someone else wearing a stripe give them a lovely compliment. HAPPY STRIPY DAY!

AUGUST 24TH

Now I am sure there are many introverts reading this. I am one. And once I realized and understood that I was an introvert, it changed everything for me. Do you need your own space? Prefer working alone? Find open-plan offices difficult? Find parties draining and often don't want to go to them?

WATCH THIS TED TALK – Susan Cain: "The Power of Introverts". If only I had heard this when I was younger. There is no need to feel "wrong" or "silly" for not being outgoing all the time. You are most likely a creative genius of some kind! Really . . .

• •

AUGUST 25TH

Conflict and disagreement can be very challenging. I hate it. But pick your battles – when it's something you know is trivial, don't overreact.

Instead, say or sing, 'You say tomato – I say tomato. Let's call the whole thing off!' And laugh the disagreement off. I challenge you to get this sentence in as many times as you can today.

NOTE: To celebrate saying this sentence you can put on the song. It's from the musical *Shall We Dance*. And it's a great YouTube video to watch for the full routine – Fred and Ginger on roller skates. What's not to love?

125

AUGUST 26TH

Hymns used to be more a part of life with regular church service attendance. You don't have to be religious to enjoy a good old-fashioned hymn sung at the top of your lungs. A lovely Dollop of Such Fun. Nay, a *rousing* Dollop of Such Fun.

Wake up and remember a hymn. Suggestion: **Morning Has Broken**, *or* **Dear Lord and Father of Mankind** *or* **All Things Bright and Beautiful**. *Wake up your loved ones by singing it to them as loud as you dare.*

NOTE: When filming, I often make a big entrance in the early hours to a make-up trailer singing *Morning Has Broken* loudly — you know, gospel-esque! I might get a hair curler thrown at me, but usually it leads to a fun group sing-a-long.

● ●

AUGUST 27TH

There are many times in my life when I have just felt stuck. Are you feeling stuck in a rut? Stuck in your relationship, in work, in ill health? It's a horrible feeling. Here's a silly way to help you out of your stuck-ness.

Don't stick, TWIST! Today is all about twisting in whatever ways you can. Wake up, put a song on and do the twist. Have a drink with a twist of lemon or lime. Have a Twister ice cream. Happy Twisting.

AUGUST 28TH

I remember seeing my little niece in a dress, twirling around, and then saying, 'Look how beautiful I am!' I wish us adults could have moments of feeling and knowing how precious we are. Yesterday was about twisting . . .

Today is about TWIRLING! Wear an outfit that is good for twirling. Twirl before you head out of the door. Make it make you feel special. Whenever you go to the toilet today, twirl before you come out! Have a twirl. Do a few public twirls. Affirm yourself every time you twirl.

NOTE: Men, you are not exempt from twirling. I twirl in jeans! I want a video of an alpha male twirling. In fact, that can be another quest for you today – persuade a man who isn't inclined to twirling to twirl! We need to free up the lads!

● ●

AUGUST 29TH

Supermarket till operators are faced with people all day and often have to work on holidays, providing you with your August Bank Holiday shopping.

Have a nice chat with your till operator. Ask them how they are. Compliment them. Maybe even buy them a little some-thing as part of your shopping! Show them appreciation and give them faith in us normally far-too-busy humans.

YOU'RE AMAZING.

AUGUST 30TH

Me and a friend have a game we like to play called, "In the style of . . ." We will say, 'Please pass me the salt, in the style of . . .' and then give a suggestion, like, the Queen or, someone very drunk who has just won the lottery, or, an excited elephant.

Play "In the style of . . ." with friends or family. Surprise them from time to time by asking them to do something in the style of something challenging. Guaranteed giggles.

• •

AUGUST 31ST

Pick someone in your family, or a friend, and celebrate them today, for no other reason than just for who they wonderfully are.

Have a Formula One winning celebration. Shake up a bottle of something fizzy (big bottle of fizzy water saves the Prosecco, I say!). Name what you want to celebrate in your friend or family member (their new hair, the way the smile, how kind they are), open the top and, as it sprays everywhere, whoop and cheer this person. Make them feel like a winner.

SEPTEMBER

• •

SEPTEMBER 1ST

The shift into September can be tricky, as the back to school feeling is around the corner. So let's make a plan to look forward to. Planning something makes you feel like you are in control and making some good, wholesome choices over your life.

Plan something for a few weeks, even months ahead. Actually book it. Have you always wanted to take your friend to the theatre? Book it! Give her/him the date. Do you want a holiday to look forward to? Book it! Have you always wanted to take the family to the seaside for the day? Book it! Plan the week-end, book the train. Basically – make a LOVELY PLAN.

SEPTEMBER 2ND

BALLS! Children can have hours of fun with their balls. As it very much were. Sometimes men more naturally muck about with theirs – again, AS IT VERY MUCH WERE.

Play with some balls (WILL YOU STOP IT!). Stress balls. Play a game of catch. Kick a ball about, even if you never have done it in your life before. Organize a game of rounders. PLAY WITH BALLS!

• •

SEPTEMBER 3RD

Animals again today. This time not just pets.

Take photos of as many animals as you can. As you take them, look at how in the moment and alive they really are. Look how sweet and special they are. Well, you are even more special and important than that. So there! Weren't thinking that, were you?

NOTE: There is no shame in playing and singing tunes from *The Lion King* on an animal day. SUCH FUN.

SEPTEMBER 4TH

If you're feeling stuck emotionally, free up your body and you might just unstick your mind from that stuck-ness. Our bodies like to be in movement so let's be kind to them and do that.

At least 3 times today walk backwards for 10 paces. You could try and have a conversation with someone as they walk forwards and you walk backwards in front of them. You could moonwalk. You could even attempt a backwards run. Walk backwards but think forwards into happier emotions. Ooh, meta!

● ●

SEPTEMBER 5TH

It's going back to school time. Jolly your usual route to work or school.

Link arms with a friend and skip along singing, 'We're off to see the Wizard, the wonderful Wizard of Oz, because, because, because, because, becauuuussssse of the wonderful things he does.'

NOTE: You can always substitute 'Wizard of Oz' for the place or person you are off to see. More jolly.

SEPTEMBER 6TH

Do you get intimidated by people? Feel nervous about things like public speaking? Imagine people look down on you? There's an old trick for that . . .

IMAGINE EVERYONE NAKED! An amusing, albeit possibly horrifying thought, and apologies because now I have made the suggestion you won't be able not to do it! But hopefully you will feel less intimidated. We're all naked underneath the bravado (and clothes).

NOTE: There is a great saying, 'Don't compare your insides with someone's outsides.' That is, it's easy to imagine someone is together and happy and in control because they look well presented and are acting confident. But actually you don't have a clue what's going on underneath. They may be feeling just as awkward and scared as you.

● ●

SEPTEMBER 7TH

Don't you just HATE junk mail? Not even our desperate 'Please no junk mail' signs help. It only adds to a stressful day.

Write some handwritten, colourful anonymous notes with nice messages on them and post through letterboxes of people you know or don't know. Let's spread cheer amongst the junk.

SEPTEMBER 8TH

Yesterday I spoke of junk as in junk mail. I tell you who has to deal with a lot of junk – bin men. Bin men courageously deal with all our rubbish.

Brighten up a bin man's day. Give him a kiss or a handshake and say, 'Thanks for clearing up our rubbish, it's really appreciated. Have a lovely day.'

SEPTEMBER 9TH

As the freedom of summer fades, are the old negative thought patterns beginning to ruminate? I hope not. But if they are, remember we are doing these fun and silly things every day to help stop giving them airtime.

Speak in rhyme as often as you can. See how long it takes people to notice. See if you can answer a question with a rhyme. You could always go a bit rappy with it! Or just rhyme in your head. HAVE FUN TIMES WITH YOUR RHYMES – which is indeed a RHYME. SUCH FUN!

SEPTEMBER 10TH

Here is another good mind distraction game. I often find my thoughts can come in on themselves at the end of the day before bedtime when I am less distracted.

Watch TV, alone or with someone, and occasionally press pause and guess what they are going to say next. Or come up with a silly answer. Best done with soaps or very serious drama, I find.

• •

SEPTEMBER 11TH

Have a little mull on this quote today.

'The whole point of being alive is to evolve into the complete person you were intended to be.' Oprah Winfrey.

Good old Oprah. She's right. Don't let your life go by without doing what is in your heart to be done. Don't let the fear of what other people think get in your way.

Write down some small ways you can move towards your goals.

SEPTEMBER 12TH

Following on from yesterday and your goals. Is there something you know is in your heart to do and you don't know where to begin?

Find an expert in that field and ask them if you can pick their brains. You may not know one, so google them and write them an email or letter. They will be thrilled to be able to help you – experts love talking about their work.

● ●

SEPTEMBER 13TH

Now, to distract you from any worries about not achieving your goals (you will, don't fret), here's a silly one for today. Why is it only children, tribal leaders and sports fans who are allowed to walk around freely with face paints?

Plan a day, if not today, when you can face paint with some friends or family and boldly spend the day with your face paint of choice. Go shopping as a tiger . . . especially if you are over 40. Brilliant.

SEPTEMBER 14TH

I spent way too many years saying, 'I really want to do a dance class.' I knew I wanted to, but felt scared, or tired, or too busy, or whatever excuse I could come up with to avoid it. Hobbies are important for us as adults (they break up the automatic busy stress patterns of life). If you like the idea of dancing . . .

Find a local dance class. Take some mates along. Go wild at the back of the class. Or, if nothing else, try and copy the routines when you watch Strictly! *After me now with the theme tune: 'De de de de de de de, de de de de de.' Lovely.*

NOTE: Think about what other hobbies you miss or would love to do. Get play back in your life.

●●●●●●●●●●●●●●●●●●●●●●●●●●●●●●●●

SEPTEMBER 15TH

People used to say to me, 'How are you feeling?' and I would answer, 'Bit tired, slight headache, but OK.' But that's not *feelings*. That's physical ailments. Get in touch with what's going on underneath.

Assign an emotion to everything you do today. Even if it feels a negative emotion, it's how you are feeling and that's OK. It will pass. You can say them aloud or to yourself.

As the toast pops up: joy. If it burns: anger. Walking to work in the rain: frustration. Decide to gallop: surprise and hope.

SEPTEMBER 16TH

Simply a reminder – you are fabulous.

Put on the cheesiest song that has possibly ever been recorded – Chesney Hawkes I am the one and only! (LOVE IT) – and claim your uniqueness. You could enter a room singing, 'I am the one and only.' It's how I like to come on stage!

NOTE: Cherishing yourself is not arrogant or selfish. Being kind to and nourishing yourself makes it possible for you to do the work you need to do. It's therefore essential. What use are you when you are exhausted and run down? None, I say, none.

● ●

SEPTEMBER 17TH

Do you like apples? Maybe you just prefer cider? NAUGHTY. But this time of year the apples are being harvested. Get in touch with your inner farmer!

Pick some apples off a tree. Or, if that's not possible, buy some seasonal and local cooking apples. And STEW! Make stewed apples. And blackberries, perhaps? YUM. You will be eating off the land. And to make it sillier, do farmer impressions all day. 'Ooh ar, my lovelies.' 'Let's make hay, eh?' Walk about with some straw in your mouth. Wear wellies for no reason. HAPPY FARMING DAY!

SEPTEMBER 18TH

Aside from our designated treat days (oh how fun they are) too much junk food really does affect the mind. Especially that nasty, addictive beast that is sugar. Back to fruit . . .

Enjoy your food before you eat it by learning to juggle with it. Oranges, apples, lemons. It doesn't take long to learn – find someone to teach you or look online. Happy juggling.

● ●

SEPTEMBER 19TH

Here's a very easy way to overcome fears and gather some courage, especially if you are superstitious.

Search for ladders on the street today and deliberately walk UNDER them. DARING! Perhaps even stand under one and do a little jig, cheer up the builders.

SEPTEMBER 20TH

'Be kind to unkind people, they need it the most.' Do you know that quote? I truly believe that tricky people are often deeply hurting more than we think.

Make or a buy a cup of tea for the person in your workplace or school who people find difficult. Or the one who is unpopular. Have a little chat with them. You never know, it might be the start of them softening.

● ●

SEPTEMBER 21ST

Well, hello to you 21st September. Which reminds me of the song *September* by Earth, Wind & Fire. So . . .

Get 21st September off to a good start and have a jolly family bop to September *by Earth, Wind & Fire.*

SEPTEMBER 22ND

A calmer September song for your amusement today.

Put on Try to Remember *– you'll get some wonderfully cheesey footage of Nana Mouskouri and Harry Belafonte!*

NOTE: The first lyrics are 'Try to remember the kind of September when life was slow and oh, so mellow.' Let that be a reminder to, well, slow and mellow . . .

● ●

SEPTEMBER 23RD

My dog often reminds me to stretch. Dogs and cats wouldn't dream of waking up and not having a good old stretch. We should too. Keeping our body nice and loose to stop any build up of tension.

It's STRETCH DAY! Have a lovely stretch when you get up. Arms to the ceiling, big yawn. Shake everything out. Throughout the day, regularly stand up and stretch it all out. Do some sports stretches if you know any. If not, arms above you, in front of you, shake them out. Try and touch your toes (don't push it if you can't), flex and move your ankles. STRETCH AWAY.

NOTE: I once stretched at work in a pair of ageing trousers and they split right down the, well, forgive me, crack. Yup. Thank goodness I hadn't decided to go commando that day. Thought this is information you would like. You're welcome.

SEPTEMBER 24TH

Keeping on the stretching theme today, continue to regularly stretch, but let's have more fun with it.

Do regular big wide arm stretches with a yawn in front of people, and see who catches the yawn. Yawns are catching – FACT. Funny to go around making people yawn!

● ●

SEPTEMBER 25TH

A little way to perk up your working environment or home. But every little bit of such fun helps.

Put out some bowls of nice nibbles! There's no reason to keep nibbles for a special occasion. Pop some cherries in a bowl, M&M's, some nuts, olives. Scatter today with lovely bowls of nibbles for people. Happy Nibble Day! (sounds wrong).

SEPTEMBER 26TH

Ladies (and those men that may sport them), I want to discuss TIGHTS. Personally, they drive me MAD. And, as we know, ONE SIZE DOES NOT FIT ALL!

After a long day, make yourself laugh for a moment and MOONWALK OUT OF YOUR TIGHTS! If you have a partner, put on the show for them.

• •

SEPTEMBER 27TH

A fun challenge for today.

Leap into a revolving door with a complete stranger! You'll have to do funny little steps in time with the door as it revolves and get amusingly close to them, too. Walk off wishing them a happy day.

SEPTEMBER 28TH

As I am sure you know by now, I love the movie *Dirty Dancing*. What's not to love? The final song is, of course, 'I've had the time of my life.'

After an event today, perhaps a meal, a meeting, a coffee or a class, go up to the person you were with or who hosted the event and sing or say, 'Thank you . . . I've had the time of my life, and I owe it all to YOU . . .'

NOTE: If appropriate, you could study the end dance of this film and do a few dance moves with the person, too.

● ●

SEPTEMBER 29TH

Feeling frustrated or pent up? Just all out of sorts? Before you resort to the usual patterns of, say, a drink, some food, or telly, simply . . .

Go for a walk. Go for a really brisk walk in the fresh air, come rain or shine, for at least half an hour. Let all that frustration fall behind you, check in with how you are feeling, where your thoughts are. Every step you make say you are making strides to move ahead with your life in a healthy way. You'll really deserve a nice sit down and a cuppa when you get in. And you might even see something fun and distracting as you walk. (No walking and texting allowed!)

SEPTEMBER 30TH

A key part of our culture is a nice cup of tea, a piece of cake and a chat. It's one of the greatest joys of being British to my mind. Life-affirming, calming, a good way to take time out.

Bake something. And give it to someone you know is or might be lonely (perhaps an elderly neighbour?) and see if they want to share a slice with you over a cuppa and a natter. And if you have never baked before – have fun popping your baking cherry. Perhaps by baking something with cherries!

NOTE: If you don't have time to bake, permission granted to purchase a baked item, it's the lovely cuppa and natter that's important here.

● ●

OCTOBER

OCTOBER 1ST

It's the beginning of another month. Golly, time moves on. But remember, you are as young as you feel. Not as SOMEONE you feel, though that's an option, but as YOU feel. Don't you feel immediately younger and freer when someone thinks you look younger than you are?

If you think someone looks a little down, politely ask them their age. Reply with a 'Wow, you look SO much younger than that. You are so youthful.' It will make them SO happy.

OCTOBER 2ND

You know when someone waves at you and you don't recognize them, so you gingerly wave back to be polite. And then you look behind you and realize they are waving at the person behind you? Always awkward. But let's not forget the joy of the wave.

Wave at someone you don't know. A big smiley wave. You may want to say, 'Yes, it is you. I think you look fab so I just wanted to wave at you. Have a nice day.' If you feel too shy to wave to a stranger, do it to someone you know, from a distance. Nothing nicer than a heart-warming wave.

● ●

OCTOBER 3RD

Cash machine queues can be one of life's little annoyances. Not with Miranda's way to jolly them up. Oh no. There's no point letting the things we can't change get us stressed.

Start a cash machine sing-a-long. 'Everybody join in . . .' and start singing Abba's Money, Money, Money. *OBVIOUSLY. (You could always play it on your phone if you don't quite dare to start a sing-a-long.)*

OCTOBER 4TH

One to jolly up shopping. This idea is best if you are over 40 but works for everyone.

Go to a clothes shop that plays loud music. State the fact – 'Sorry, are we shopping or bopping? Is this a disco?' And start dancing.

NOTE: If you are a parent with a young teenager, ideally do this with them to REALLY embarrass them. SUCH FUN.

● ●

OCTOBER 5TH

A challenge to break your normal morning routine. Set that fun tone for the rest of the day.

GO THREE-LEGGED WITH SOMEONE ON YOUR WAY TO SCHOOL OR WORK! Do a celebratory gallop once you are untied and arrive at your destination. Or you could have a three-legged race in your lunch break. Channel the freedom of youth.

OCTOBER 6TH

Variety is the spice of life. Do you need inspiration to vary your diet? Look no further.

Eat only things that could fit through a letterbox! Ham, salami, cheese, sliced tomato – the list is endless if you think about it. At the end of the day post some food through a neighbour's letterbox! But not soup, because that would be mean.

• •

OCTOBER 7TH

Family is important, however difficult those relationships might be. Put the difficulty aside, if you can, because we are all just broken people doing our best. There was a study that followed people from their college years into their 80s to see what defined their happiness. The answer was: trusted relationships. Not money, not fame, but relationships.

Ring your mum, or dad, aunt, grandparent or siblings. Just for a chat. If you are stuck for conversation, talk about me!

Mark Twain said: 'There isn't time, so brief is life, for bickerings, apologies, heartburnings, callings to account. There is only time for loving . . .'

OCTOBER 8TH

It's easy to feel out of control and overwhelmed by life. The thought of that To Do list and how much you are juggling. Do a small thing to take a break and get yourself feeling centred and under control.

Organize your sock drawer! May sound boring but it's very satisfying. Throw the holey ones away. See if any of the single ones match. Buy yourself a new pair of socks to celebrate an organized sock drawer.

NOTE: I distinctly remember a morning I was feeling physically run down with anxiety and I made my bed and tidied my room and felt instantly more in control. It can work.

● ●

OCTOBER 9TH

On a sock drawer theme again!

Put something funny or surprising in a loved one's sock drawer! Make them smile when they find either a nice 'for no reason other than you love them' present, or something ridiculous like a pineapple.

NOTE: You can also do this with shoes – put something silly in someone's shoes. LARKS.

OCTOBER 10TH

CRAFTS! There is a reason crafts are recommended for calming people with nervous system disorders. They are lovely distractions and bring out your creativity, thereby shutting off the analyzing, over-thinking side of your brain. And they are enjoyable whether you are feeling anxious or not.

Don't BE crafty, GET crafty! If you don't have the time and resources to do something big and fun like papier maché, or knitting, or tapestry, or Lego, then do whatever you can – make a little dog out of Blu Tack in the office. Make a paper aeroplane. Press a flower. Do a little drawing. Do something nice 'n' crafty.

● ●

OCTOBER 11TH

Here's a Dose of Such Fun again on the craft theme. Oh yes I do love me some CRAFTS!

Make a necklace out of something holey (e.g. Hula Hoops/ Polos/pasta). Snack on it throughout the day (though perhaps not if the pasta is uncooked). Or present it to someone in a lovely box and insist they wear it for the day.

OCTOBER 12TH

We can learn so much from the older generations, yet they are often overlooked.

Think of someone older who you may know (have you spoken to your gran recently?); or you could even approach someone you haven't met before, and ask them about their lives. What do they miss about the generation they grew up in? What would be the best piece of advice they could give the younger generation today? They will be THRILLED to feel valued and you may learn something invaluable.

● ●

OCTOBER 13TH

Autumn is very much here. And you know what we haven't done? Our seasonal AUTUMN GALLOP!

You know what to do: GALLOP IN A PUBLIC PLACE! Feel the child-like joy and freedom of the gallop.

NOTE: You can always ramp this season's gallop up by getting some speakers to blare out the theme tune to *Black Beauty* so everyone can join in with you.

OCTOBER 14TH

Another one for parents of teenagers. Sorry to be specific today and rule others out but we all know that parenting teenagers can be pretty tough at times.

Give teenagers a taste of their own medicine. Come in from work, kick your shoes off leaving them in the hallway, go straight to the fridge, drink something from the carton, eat something standing in front of it, storm upstairs, slam your bedroom door, put on some '70s or '80s music really loudly, then storm downstairs and demand they give you 20 quid. FUN!

NOTE: If you don't have children, or your children are older or younger, you can still behave like a teenager – you'll just have to demand 20 quid off yourself! And if you are a teenager, do some Dad Dancing.

• •

OCTOBER 15TH

Instead of getting fed up with the weather, embrace the bad elements because they will soon pass. You can see your thoughts like the weather – a bad thought can come in but just think, 'No, not going to get sucked into that negativity. It's just a thought that will pass like a storm, and the sun will come out again soon.' That's a simple version of mindfulness. So today it's embracing the elements.

Put on the song Weather With You *and dance in whatever weather is presenting itself. If it's windy, let it blow all your troubles away. Do a Windy Dance (hopefully just windy meteorologically and not digestively, but anything goes).*

OCTOBER 16TH

Want a new fun way to treat a friend or loved one?

Get home before they do and create a spa at home. Put on some calming spa music, have a tub of warm water and soapy bubbles ready for them to put their feet into. Give them a foot massage. Play the spa therapist and ask them how their day was. Perhaps do a pedicure, or manicure, or even a back massage. Run them a bath. Get some post-treatment camomile tea. A SPA AT HOME – NICE!

●●●●●●●●●●●●●●●●●●●●●●●●●●●●●●●●

OCTOBER 17TH

I have suggested air drums as a good way to start a day. But today . . .

It's AIR GUITAR DAY! Put on a good song for air guitar. (I suggest Dire Straits – because then you can air guitar knowing you are NOT in dire straits – do you see what I did there?) Instigate a group air-guitar moment at work or school. Dare you to do some public air guitar whilst listening to an iPod.

NOTE: If you actually play the guitar, then actually play the guitar today!

OCTOBER 18TH

You must have seen the musical *Grease*? (If not, your challenge for the day is to watch *Grease*.)

Have a GREASE DAY! Instead of saying, 'What a great idea!' or when giving a compliment to someone who is looking hot today, use the sentences 'My chills are multiplying' and 'I am losing control!' Have a group sing-a-long to Summer Loving. *Adopt the smooth swagger of Danny and Rizzo. Shoulders back, pecks out. Do a Danny hairbrush or comb move. GO GREASE!*

● ●

OCTOBER 19TH

Yesterday I mentioned adopting the swagger of Danny in *Grease*. Adopting a strong pose sends those messages to your brain. You feel sad and anxious if you hunch forward, cross your arms and droop your head.

Adopt a power stance that makes you feel strong and capable. Your own unique super hero stance. Whenever you feel weak today, put your body in this pose. I promise you it works.

NOTE: When I started to put my shoulders back and open up my chest, even though my anxiety didn't want me to, it was a key part of my getting better.

OCTOBER 20TH

Just to remind you – all my Daily Doses of Such Fun are for a reason. To try and get you to think about something else, break any fears or negative thought habits. Stop you feeling crazy. But talking of crazy . . .

Find some crazy paving, and go crazy on the crazy paving. Walk normally as you approach it, go crazy on it, walk normally off it. People will think you are crazy but you'll know you are doing something to stop you feeling crazy. SUCH FUN.

● ●

OCTOBER 21ST

As we all know, sport is excellent for emotional health. Not only great as exercise, but as a brilliant mental distraction, and brings a sense of community. But sport is not for everyone, and it's easy to feel intimidated by the fit people or athletes.

Make up your own new sport that is perfect for you. If you can't think of one and would like to use mine it's, wait for it, Dry Land Synchronized Swimming. I know – genius. Ideally wearing rubber armbands and a rubber ring, but essentially just doing synchronized swimming moves whilst standing, kneeling or on the floor. It's a cross between dance and swimming. I am planning to make it an Olympic sport.

OCTOBER 22ND

Writing can be so cathartic. Just getting all your emotions down on paper can be really releasing. Any budding writers reading this?

If you want to see your name in print – how about writing to a newspaper about an issue you believe in and see if they will publish it. When you write your letter, take on the guise of a proper writer – sit in a café with a beret and scarf, perhaps. Have an eccentric creative day today.

NOTE: If writing is not your thing, how about phoning into a local or national radio. Something weirdly exciting about hearing yourself on the radio waves.

• •

OCTOBER 23RD

I always feel envious that children have a book day at school.

Adults – dress up as a character from your favourite book and assume that character for the day. If you are going to choose Fifty Shades of Grey *please don't inflict that on the rest of us! Perhaps organize a book day at your place of work – some-one's boss might be Fagan. All sorts of larks might occur.*

OCTOBER 24TH

Ever feel like you are in the rat race of life? Well step away from that thought because life isn't a race and all our lives go at a different pace. Don't compare yourself to other people. Take the gas off.

Get some friends and family in a park or garden, and have a race – but it's the slowest person who wins. You have to keep moving, but as slowly as you can. Who's going to be the tortoise?

NOTE: When I was unwell, I had to keep saying to myself, 'There is no deadline to be well' and take all pressure off. It's a good mantra for those with long-term problems and those who push themselves.

● ●

OCTOBER 25TH

The leaves on the trees are falling. I find I can easily get down as winter approaches. But let's not mourn the passing summer and the light evenings, autumn can be a time for family, friends, getting things done, and cosy nights in. It's all good. So embrace and celebrate autumn.

Go into the garden or park and try and catch falling leaves as they drop from the trees. I used to do this with my sister and my cousins when we were younger and doing it as an adult always brings me cheer.

OCTOBER 26TH

It's officially autumn when there are piles of leaves around. If you are still struggling to embrace the colder months ahead, don't worry, the rest of autumn and winter have plenty of fun options for you.

Find a pile of leaves. Kick them. Hear their rustles. Or dive in and have a roll around. Or have a leaf fight. A leaf never hurt anyone. Just move away from those conkers. Though you could go bonkers with conkers . . .

● ●

OCTOBER 27TH

I am often saying 'Anything goes' – all part of freeing us up, not feeling judged, and being true to ourselves.

Put on the fabulous showtune that is Anything Goes. *Do some fake tap dancing – I like to do that. I pretend I am a genius tap dancer. And, remember, today 'anything goes'.*

NOTE: There is no point fearing what others think of you, you are only guessing what they are thinking anyway and you are 99.9 per cent certain to be wrong. Let go of worrying what others think.

OCTOBER 28TH

Today I want to set a relatively big challenge. Treat yourself but also feel free and empowered. This is a great challenge for the more shy amongst you who fear what people think.

DINE ALONE. You may think people are looking at you – they aren't. You just look like a carefree confident person having a meal. So believe that you are. Take a book or some work you need to catch up on. POWER TO YOU – you are DINING ALONE.

● ●

OCTOBER 29TH

Welcome to Miranda's (for no reason at all) ITALIAN DAY!

GO ITALIAN! Say 'Ciao'*. Call everyone* Bellissima*. Use more hand and arm gestures than normal. Have a pizza or a big bowl of pasta. Watch* The Italian Job. *Have a pannacotta. Put on some opera. Have some lovely Italian moments.*

OCTOBER 30TH

The clocks must have recently gone backwards so . . .

It's time for the TIME WARP dance from the The Rocky Horror Show *again. Dance into the Winter Time . . .*

● ●

OCTOBER 31ST

It's Halloween. I don't mean to be a party pooper, but I am NOT a fan. Sorry. Why are we getting in touch with horrid ghosts and ghouls? Too spooky. Not good for anxious souls.

Dress up like a children's entertainer or clown – something jolly! Lots of bright colours. Knock on people's doors and give THEM a sweetie. Be the jolly face of Halloween!

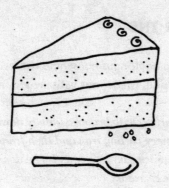

NOVEMBER

● ●

NOVEMBER 1ST

Want to feel better in the morning? Want to FEEL GOOD? Here is a fun way to put a positive message into your system for the first day of a new month.

First thing in the morning, put on Nina Simone's **Feeling Good.** *Let it seep into your every pore so you end up FEELING GOOD. Such a great song.*

NOTE: For added fun, I tend do a high-leg-kicking performance down the stairs before ending in a dramatic pose as I pop the kettle on.

NOVEMBER 2ND

Dreading those monotonous household chores? Don't worry, they needn't be dull. Oh no, not with me around . . .

Do imaginary curling with brooms. Ideally down a corridor. Throw an imaginary curling iron and then frantically polish and brush away. Such fun. This can also be done in school, hospital or office corridors.

NOTE: I know this is possible because I *have* done it in an office! Unfortunately, I didn't realize the CEO of the company was heading towards me as I frantically broom curled away. But there's not much a boss can say to, 'Sorry, I was just doing some imaginary curling.'

●●●●●●●●●●●●●●●●●●●●●●●●●●●●●●●

NOVEMBER 3RD

I know I repeat myself about the importance of healthy eating. I just care about you, that's all. But as this is a book of Daily Doses of FUN my food ideas focus on treating ourselves. (Remember the 80/20 rule – 80 per cent healthy/20 per cent treats.)

It's Create an Unusual Snack Day! Why not slice open a big marshmallow and pop in a chocolate button or Malteser? Or go savoury and put some Twiglets into a sandwich for extra crunch factor. Be creative on SNACK DAY.

NOTE: Healthier snack day options – roll a carrot baton in a slice of ham that has been spread with mustard. Anything goes.

NOVEMBER 4TH

Now this idea has amused me as I've been writing, but I just don't know if it's too hard to do . . . Do let me know if you succeed.

Become the driver of an imaginary bus. Pick up people along the way saying, 'Anyone want to come aboard my imaginary bus down the street?' Make car noises. Sing The Wheels on the Bus go Round and Round. *When people have to get off to go in another direction wave them a lovely goodbye. IT MUST BE POSSIBLE! A gathering of people moving together on an imaginary bus. I want to see it!*

● ●

NOVEMBER 5TH

Do you spend enough time as a family or with the friends who you live with? Or are you often watching TV in separate rooms? It's important to spend time together. Remember, being in relationships is essential for happiness.

Choose a TV programme to watch together. Write down some silly things to say or do and put them in a bowl. Give each other a word (a common enough word so it's likely to come up in the TV programme) and every time that word is said during the programme, that person has to pick a thing to do from the bowl and do it. SUCH FUN TIMES AHEAD.

NOVEMBER 6TH

Now I know I mention the joys of film and television a lot. They are, of course, wondrous art forms and provide education, entertainment and escapsim, especially on dark winter nights. But today . . .

Have a non-screen day. Have a READING day and night instead. It's easy to forget the joy of a book in our age of easy access to the screen.

As Matt Haig, who has lived with anxiety and depression and is the author of Reasons to Stay Alive, *says:*

'. . . books. They were, in and of themselves, reasons to stay alive. Every book written is the product of a human mind in a particular state. Add all the books together and you get the end sum of humanity. Every time I read a great book I felt I was reading a kind of map, a treasure map, and the treasure I was being directed to was in actual fact myself.'

So, HAPPY READING! Perhaps try a classic you have never read.

NOVEMBER 7TH

Feeling the need for some privacy? Is the house feeling a bit overwhelmingly busy? Do what a child might do . . .

MAKE A DEN! Hang a bedspread from a bed to a piece of furniture. Hang a sheet over it for walls. Sit in it and have a lovely cuppa! Or get adventurous and make one outside betwixt trees 'n' bushes.

NOVEMBER 8TH

How's your sleep going? Don't you envy those people who hit the pillow and are out like a light? SO ANNOYING OF THEM! I take a lot longer to, what I call, wind down.

Have a candlelit night. Buy loads of little tea lights (you can get them very cheaply) and scatter them all over the sitting room, bedroom and kitchen. Or choose one room if it's tricky to put them everywhere. Use a torch to move between rooms. Very calming and a much better way to wind down pre-sleep sleeps!

• •

NOVEMBER 9TH

Yesterday I suggested candlelight to help you wind down before beddy-byes. Did you know that screens can stimulate the brain and, of course, what you watch on TV before you go to bed can affect your mood and wind you up not down. Anyone else wound up for days after a horror?! I just can't do them.

Try to have no screen watching of any kind for the hour before bed. Read, chat, play a game, listen to music, do some gentle exercise – find other ways to calm yourself. I am going to suggest you all get into your pyjamas and sit on the bed together listing your favourite things, like that scene in The Sound Of Music.

NOVEMBER 10TH

Am I alone in thinking there is something inherently funny about root vegetables. Probably. They look like they could be aliens – TURNIPS. Let's have a root vegetable day.

Try and get the word PARSNIP into a conversation – you could do this with a work colleague. It might lighten up an otherwise dull meeting. You could continue your root vegetable day by having roast parsnips and carrots for dinner (I don't know what you do with turnips). Yum. Or dress them up as aliens! Pop them on someone's pillow and film the reaction. (Oh how childish, I hear you say. Me? Childish?)

● ●

NOVEMBER 11TH

Don't you just LOVE getting into bed after a long and tiring day? It's the best thing. Never take it for granted. And if you don't know my trick for getting into a cold bed on a Winter Night . . .

Do the COLD BED DANCE! Shimmy on those sheets, cause friction and get warmed up. It's the horizontal dance of bed loving!

NOVEMBER 12TH

Some of the things I suggest to jolly your life up and break negative cycles may seem dotty, but don't judge them or yourselves. Celebrate the fun and freedom they bring.

Have a DOTTY DAY! Wear something dotty. Eat something dotty (holey cheese anyone?). Drink out of a mug with dots on it. Look out for all things dotty. If you see someone else wearing a dot then give them a compliment. HAPPY DOTTY DAY!

● ●

NOVEMBER 13TH

Another idea for not forgetting the healing properties of our gorgeous pets.

Spend 10 minutes doing exactly what your pet is doing at this moment (unless it's licking its bottom). Is it sleeping, stretching, breathing nice and deeply, pottering around, or running? Whatever it's doing will be a nice thing for you to do (again, unless it's licking its bottom).

NOVEMBER 14TH

Simple task today. But it needs a bit of courage!

Treat yourself to a nice bun, piece of cake or brownie. In public. As you bite into it say as loudly and poshly as you dare, 'Oh, good lord, that's MOIST!'

● ●

NOVEMBER 15TH

Today's task is another fun way to cherish your loved ones.

Make up a cheerleading song (dance optional) for a loved one as they get home. Or for a friend when you greet them. This is one of mine:

'Two, Four, Six, Eight, who do we appreciate? Mum, yes Mum, lovely Mum, yummy Mum, go Mum, go Mum! Now can I get you anything for your tum?'

SUCH FUN.

NOTE: Pompoms are very much encouraged.

NOVEMBER 16TH

Do you wake up thinking about the worries of the day before you think about your loved ones? Do you reach for your phone before you greet them?

Put on the song Lovely Day *by Bill Withers. Surprise your loved one, turn over and sing the section: 'Then I look at you, and the world's all right with me, just one look at you, and I know it's going to be, a lovely day . . .' AAAAAAHHHH!*

NOTE: Please just *speak* the lyrics if your singing would ruin the moment! Also, if you suffer from morning breath, perhaps have a quick teeth brush . . .

● ●

NOVEMBER 17TH

We are SO busy in this generation. Life is at such a pace. There is so much noise. So much clamouring for our attention. And most of us have some level of addiction to our smartphones.

Switch your phone off. Sit for 10 minutes in complete silence. On your own. CAN YOU IMAGINE SUCH A THING? Then at the end, write down the main thoughts you were having. You might just learn what's going on with you without all the noise. Brave it. You might come up with the most amazing idea that will change your life.

NOVEMBER 18TH

I wouldn't normally advocate practical jokes that give people a fright, but I think this one is worth it!

Strike a freeze pose next to a mannequin in a shop window, or do a freeze pose in your home window, or office window if it faces on to a street. As people walk past, suddenly move and boo them!

NOTE: Sometimes getting a fun fright is no bad thing for people feeling low or wanting to hide. It wakes you up and makes you feel alive. So don't feel bad. But maybe don't pick on someone looking frail!

. . . .

NOVEMBER 19TH

Winter is approaching. Are you feeling tired? Is life feeling heavy? Do you feel like you are wading through treacle at the moment? I hope not. But if so . . .

Cheer yourself up and buy some treacle. Don't wade through it – you could, but it would be exceptionally messy. Google some recipes you can make with treacle and make a lovely treacle something. Lovely word – treacle. You could always try and get it into a conversation today. TREACLE. Perhaps call someone treacle.

NOVEMBER 20TH

One of my favourite films is *Truly, Madly, Deeply*. Today I am suggesting doing something they did in a scene.

Gaze at the clouds. See if you can see a shape in one of them – a person, an animal, an object. Perhaps there may be one that looks like someone you know. Happy cloud gazing. Aren't they amazing?

● ●

NOVEMBER 21ST

Today I want to remind you how special you are. Is it perhaps a quarter or half birthday of yours today? Good excuse for a little celebration. Children always tell you exactly how old they are – I am 8 and a HALF, or I am 6 and a QUARTER. Let's do that, too!

Make a note of your half birthday date. On that day, and practise it today, remind yourself that you are here on this planet as a unique person, with unique gifts and a unique purpose. You have to believe that – because it is absolute fact. Not convinced? Then remember this: THERE IS NO ONE ELSE ON THIS PLANET LIKE YOU. THERE IS ONLY ONE YOU. So you can only be but AMAZING.

NOVEMBER 22ND

Sometimes I go through phases of swearing more than normal.
I think the odd swear is wholly appropriate and oft essential.
But when you find yourself swearing a lot or more than
normal then maybe there is some anger going on below and
things are not quite right.

Get out of the swearing pattern by replacing your swear words
with bum, bosoms and bottomsticks, and anything else you can
think of beginning with 'b' that is silly. Hopefully it will make
you and others laugh and diffuse the situation.

● ●

NOVEMBER 23RD

A small thing that was a key part of my recovery from anxiety
was choosing to do a Photo of the Day every day. Every night
I would look at the photo and it would reinforce the positive
memory of that moment.

Today, search for moments that can be your Photo of the Day.
It could be as simple as a beautiful leaf. Or a selfie of you and
a friend smiling. Perhaps decide to do this every day, or at
least until the end of the year.

NOTE: I think this is one very good thing about Instagram. If
you make it about your Photo of the Day happy memory and
not about showing off about your life (don't get me started!).

NOVEMBER 24TH

Sometimes getting into a car on your own on a cold and dark morning is pretty miserable. So try perking up someone else's morning, which will, in turn, perk up yours. A perk circle!

Put an anonymous note on a random car saying: 'You are a MARVELLOUS parker and look LOVELY when you drive.'

●●●●●●●●●●●●●●●●●●●●●●●●●●●●●●●

NOVEMBER 25TH

A very silly idea to get your mind playing and distracted today.

Welcome to TALK AS SOMEONE ELSE DAY! Choose a person-ality you like and try and get their catchphrases into your everyday speech without people noticing. If you are stuck for ideas you can always try phrases from my sitcom: 'Bear with', 'Such fun', 'Hello to you', 'What have you done today to make yourself feel proud' or 'What I call'.

NOVEMBER 26TH

A well-known mindfulness technique is to do a simple habit breaker of sitting in a different chair at home to the one you normally sit in. See the room from a different angle. How about extending this and changing family dynamics?

If you are young, go old. Put on some slippers, a cardigan, perhaps, sit down slowly with a cup of hot chocolate and have a good old natter about the old days. Have a war song sing-a-long ('Pack up your troubles in your old kit bag' anyone?). If you are old, go young. Mothers and grandmothers really embarrass your kids and start rapping. Put on some Kanye West and bust some hip-hop moves. Brilliant.

NOTE: When I first heard someone talk about Kanye West I thought they were talking about a train station.

● ●

NOVEMBER 27TH

Talking of becoming old when you are young, as we were yesterday, today I am calling on the younger generation . . .

Plan or go to BINGO! Seriously. Hang out with the oldies. Get chatting. See if you can keep up – it's surprisingly hard! And SUCH FUN. Or do your own version at home, or roll out a puzzle. Go old!

NOVEMBER 28TH

Amuse yourself and others in the street by being literal today. It will help you look out for things mindfully too.

Move very, very slowly underneath a sign that says DEAD SLOW. FUNNY! Are there still Heavy Plant Crossing signs? If so, find one and carry a plant and pretend it's really heavy. Stand under a mile per hour sign if it's your age and take a photo. Stoop with an imaginary walking stick and do a doddery walk at the discriminatory Old People Crossing sign. GET LITERAL WITH SIGNS.

● ●

NOVEMBER 29TH

I am passionate about community. And it's so relevant in our ever–more-isolated technological age.

When you next make an online transaction – a supermarket shop, or clothes purchase, whatever – then chat to your computer as if it's a person. Extra points if you dare chat to your computer in public.

'Yes, I think I will have six bananas from that previous order, thank you.'

'Do I want to check out?' 'No, I think I will continue shopping first.'

'Now I am ready to check out, thank you.' 'Yes, thank you for reminding me, I would like to buy those again, I had forgotten, thank you.' 'Now I am finished.' 'Check out, please.' 'Yes I am certain, thank you.' 'Yes, I would like to confirm purchase.' 'Will you be sending me an email to confirm that?' 'Oh, how lovely, you will.' 'Thank you. Great doing business with you and have a lovely day.'

NOVEMBER 30TH

Our lives are too sedentary. Let's get moving people! We don't want any deep vein thrombosis (I had one after a knee operation once, it's not pleasant). As I've been drumming into you: energized relaxed body = energized relaxed mind.

Set an alarm on your phone for every half an hour today. When it goes off do a star jump or a dance move of your choice. Encourage your colleagues to do the same. Everyone doing a dance move every half hour could only be but SUCH FUN.

DECEMBER

• •

DECEMBER 1ST

Happy 1st December to you. Sing, 'Happy December the First to me' please. Very nice.

Buy a chocolate advent calendar. Eat all the chocolates, then close the windows!

DECEMBER 2ND

Fires are so . . . warming. Don't say I don't teach you things. But they are warming for the soul. Watching the magical flames, feeling the heat. Yummy.

Light a fire. Watch it mindfully as you still your thoughts. Sit by the fire for a bit. If you don't have a fireplace maybe think about having a bonfire, or a small fire in an oven dish in the garden. Or light a candle.

NOTE: You can still toast marshmallows on a candle. Trust me, I've mastered it.

● ●

DECEMBER 3RD

If you couldn't fire watch yesterday, or you found it hard to be mindful and your thoughts kept a-whirring, then try being mindful towards your pet – feel their fur, hear them breathe, watch intently how they move.

Take a selfie lying down with your pet. Send it to a friend who you know will like it or find it funny.

NOTE: If you have a small, fluffy pet then you can play Find a Pose That Makes Your Pet Look Like a Russian Hat. Hours of fun.

DECEMBER 4TH

Have you ever looked in the window of a bed shop and seen someone trying out a new bed? I haven't and that's always been disappointing. It would make me laugh to see it. Make someone laugh today whilst having fun yourself.

Tuck yourself into a display bed, and start sucking your thumb or sleep talking. Or get into bed with a stranger who is also trying out a bed! Now THAT would be a good way to meet the love of your life!

● ●

DECEMBER 5TH

I love Christmas but sometimes I get out the decorations and it feels a bit like a chore. It's the same old decs.

Buy a new Christmas decoration. Something that makes you smile. Don't just put up your usual decorations. How about a Santa loo seat (yes they exist!)? A singing and dancing Reindeer (yes they exist!)? Or a Christmas tree dress (yes they exist!)? Get silly with your Christmas décor.

NOTE: If budgets are tight how about picking some holly. Whilst singing The Holly and the Ivy very loudly, obviously.

DECEMBER 6TH

I do love carolling at Chrimbo. 'Tis indeed the season to be jolly. So us Daily Dosers of Such Fun are going to have a lot of laughs throughout December. Get ready.

Plan to go to a carol concert. If they do The Twelve Days of Christmas *then REALLY go for it and sing as loudly as you dare on 'FIVE GOLD RINGS'. Make the people around you laugh. Encourage them to do it. You could always have your own carol concert at home. Certainly put some carols on for a warm-up session, whether you go to a concert or not.*

•••••••••••••••••••••••••••••••

DECEMBER 7TH

Sometimes it can feel a pressure to be jolly during the Christmas season. If you aren't feeling jolly yet, here's something that might help.

Put on some carols and disco dance to them. Nothing funnier than doing some hardcore disco moves to Ding Dong Merrily on High.

DECEMBER 8TH

We only have the day we are in, so don't waste away the winter nights wishing for spring again, or letting them get you down. Make use of the long nights.

Set up a weekly film club. Think of a film you have never seen, a classic perhaps, or one you are desperate to see. Tell your friends when you are planning to have the showing. Send out formal invites – show times, running length, synopsis of the film. And, of course, GET POPCORN.

NOTE: This is something I carry on into January and February. I love it.

● ●

DECEMBER 9TH

Parents – have you just been watching your children's nativity play or taking them off to school dressed in their various outfits?

How about an adult nativity play?! Get some people round for a coffee, put tea towels over your heads, use toys as animals and baby Jesus, do paper scissors stone for who is going to be Mary and Joseph. Then get role-playing! One of you can film it so you can proudly show your children YOUR nativity play!!

DECEMBER 10TH

Finding it hard to get up in the dark? Dread opening the curtains when you just want to be in bed? Or maybe you find it hard closing the curtains as it gets dark so early? See if this helps.

Whenever you open or close curtains or blinds, do it in as theatrical a way as possible. I want lots of swishing and dramatic poses, please. When you open them say, 'Hello world, aren't you lucky to have me? Today is going to be a great day.'

NOTE: You could also play Madonna's *Vogue* while pose-striking at the window. Please put clothes on before posing, I thank you!

● ●

DECEMBER 11TH

Let's be grateful for beds again today. And celebrate CLEAN SHEET NIGHT!

If you need to change your sheets (come on, we can all leave them that little bit too long, own up), change them tonight. Pull back the duvet and dive into bed in a celebratory manner feeling the gorgeous clean sheets. Throw the duvet over yourself and have a good roll around (euphemistically or not), celebrating your lovely bed. It's CLEAN SHEET NIGHT!

DECEMBER 12TH

Some of these daily fun ideas have been aimed at reducing our isolated activity on our smartphones and devices. However, technology obviously serves a fantastic purpose and deserves to be celebrated.

Today change your ringtone, or your wallpaper photo, or screensaver. Make sure the images really inspire you and amuse you – you could always have a photo of ME! Change them regularly, too. It's something you look at more often than you realize, so changing them helps avoid the brain getting into any ruts.

●●●●●●●●●●●●●●●●●●●●●●●●●●●●●●

DECEMBER 13TH

Sometimes in December, earlier even, we can worry what we are going to do for New Year's Eve. I am not a fan of a big party on New Year's Eve, it feels like too much pressure to have the perfect night. I prefer a quiet evening at home.

Plan to do exactly what YOU WANT to do for New Year's Eve. Organize the perfect way for you to spend it. Don't bow to peer pressure.

DECEMBER 14TH

I remember once being very close to a full-blown panic attack but I found a way to stop it. So this will help if you are panicking, or just feeling like you need to have a moment of calm before your next task.

Do a detailed sketch of a household or workplace object with a pencil. Really simple – just on a postcard or in a notepad. Choose an object you are around a lot but have never really studied. It's amazing what you discover by drawing it in detail. And it can totally calm your mind as you become absorbed in the task.

PS IT'S MY BIRTHDAY TODAY. HAPPY BIRTHDAY ME!

● ●

DECEMBER 15TH

Do you feel pretty safe in your local area? The key ingredient to having a calm mind is feeling safe.

Go up to a policeman or woman today, shake their hand and say, 'Thanks for making me feel safe.' You'll make their day.

NOTE: If you want to be a bit cheeky you could do a little bob and say, 'Evening officer' old-fashioned Bobby style.

DECEMBER 16TH

Not feeling Christmassy yet? Here's a REALLY fun, what I call, idea.

Tee up the song Rock Around the Christmas Tree. *Go and find as many Christmas trees as you can, stand next to them and literally rock around the Christmas trees. My favourite Christmas song.*

• •

DECEMBER 17TH

'Christmas time, mistletoe and wine,' sing along with me now, 'Children singing, Christian rhyme . . .' Just helping you to get in a Christmas spirit. How about . . .

Plan a trip to a PANTO. Or go tonight spontaneously. Be a child again – when were you last at a Panto?

NOTE: If the answer to anything today is 'It's behind you', say it loudly and gleefully Panto style.

DECEMBER 18TH

I have got a Christmas alternative to Internet dating.

Wear a bobble hat, some antlers or some other kind of head-band and apply a piece of mistletoe to it. Look and feel as dapper as you can and, you never know, Mr or Mrs Right might just approach you for a kiss underneath your mistletoe (if you pardon).

● ●

DECEMBER 19TH

Christmas is a notoriously difficult time for people to feel lonely. We need connection even more at this time of year.

Do something you have never done before to help others this Christmas. Volunteer at a homeless shelter, for example. Or is there anyone you know who will be on their own on Christmas Day you could invite over? Do something truly kind this Christmas for someone.

DECEMBER 20TH

I declare 20th December to be *The Sound of Music* day. It's one of my favourite films and one I always bung on at Christmas.

Watch **The Sound of Music***! Learn the* **So Long, Farewell** *routine and whenever you say goodbye to friends and family for the rest of the year, burst into that song!*

● ●

DECEMBER 21ST

Welcome to the shortest day of the year. Say, 'Hello Short Day, how very short you are.' The skies are now only going to get longer – yay!

Have a short day. Wear a pair of shorts (with tights perhaps). Walk on your knees to feel shorter. If you are naturally short, claim this as YOUR day. It's a celebration of short. Make short phone calls. Have shorter meetings. Cut it all short. On the way home, take a short cut. Have a short haircut. Happy SHORT DAY!

DECEMBER 22ND

Resenting any household chores when you just want to be sitting with your feet up nursing an eggnog? You are doing a wonderful thing for your loved ones by doing the chores. Try and keep cheerful when you do them.

Put a wash on. Amuse yourself by singing at your washing, 'You spin me right round, baby, right round, like a record, baby, right round.' Or 'You're spinning around, you're out of my way, I know you're feeling me cuz you like it like this!' A Kylie song always brings cheer, me thinks. Put on The Locomotion *to move to your next chore!*

● ●

DECEMBER 23RD

HAPPY CHRISTMAS EVE EVE. The big day is nearly here. Christmas usually takes care of itself, fun wise, but here's a thought.

Prepare your own version of the Queen's speech. Make or buy a crown and write a round-up of your family's year and perform it Queen style on Christmas Day.

DECEMBER 24TH

HAPPY CHRISTMAS EVE. Excited about tomorrow?

Go to the local store or pound shop and buy some comedy Christmas hats for every member of your family. Insist they wear them at the meal tomorrow.

● ●

DECEMBER 25TH

IT'S CHRRIISSTTMMAASSSSSS! Have a wonderful, wonderful day.

I wish you a very, very merry Christmas.

NOTE: If today is difficult for you, for any reason, then think about being jolly for others, or find ways to be kind to others. Think outwards not inwards on Christmas Day if you can. Whatever you do, be kind to yourself too.

DECEMBER 26TH

HAPPY BOXING DAY! You might still be feeling full or tired from yesterday's excitements. Get yourself going.

Get boxing on Boxing Day! Put on Eye of the Tiger *or some other inspirational tune and do some* Rocky *style boxing boxes. Punch your way out of your hangover. Box on Boxing Day. Genius.*

● ●

DECEMBER 27TH

I always wish winter could be constant snow. I love snow. Snowmen, toboggans, skiing, snow boots. Bright, white and fresh. Just magical.

If it's snowing – HAVE A SNOWBALL FIGHT. If it's not snow-ing – buy some cotton wool balls. Put them in water. Have a cotton wool ball fight!

DECEMBER 28TH

There can often be a nasty lull post Christmas, I find. It's easy to feel down.

Write a list of 20 dreams. They can be as fantastical as possible. You just never know what will come true when you put them out there. And it should bring some hope and energy to the post-Christmas lull. DREAMS DO COME TRUE.

'It's kind of fun to do the impossible.' Walt Disney

● ●

DECEMBER 29TH

The sun is closer to the earth in the northern hemisphere during the winter. So when there is some sun peeping through the clouds, it provides us with vitamin D that can help our mood and energy levels.

If the sun is out today, even if you are in loads of hats and coats, sit in the winter sun for 20 minutes. Feel that lovely healing warmth on your face. If it's not out, force yourself to go outside anyway. Run around to get warm, then lie down and look at the winter sky.

DECEMBER 30TH

Have you over-indulged this season? It's very hard not to. May I suggest that one might need a slightly leaner January? However, there's no point starting now whilst indulging mode is very much on.

Before you think about reducing the Christmas intake, HAVE YOUR FAVOURITE PUDDING. Savour every mouthful. Enjoy every taste. Say to yourself as you eat it, 'I am a beautiful and good person and that's why I am treating myself to this pudding because I am NOT a pudding.' Do you see?!

• •

DECEMBER 31ST

It's 31st December. WELL DONE YOU. You have got through another year in your wonderful life. Whether it's been a good one or a tricky one, it is all part of the rich tapestry of your unique life story. And tomorrow a new story can begin.

Write down 10 things you are incredibly grateful for from this year. Pat yourself on the back (literally) for getting through the tougher times.

And remember, do what you WANT to do tonight for New Year's Eve. No pressure. HAPPY NEW YEAR!

ACKNOWLEDGMENTS

Thank you to all my dear friends, family and colleagues who have inspired me to be more positive, fun and silly and find joy despite difficult circumstances.

Particularly Bella, Lareena Brown, Gerry McNulty, Perry-May Britton, The Meldrums and Masons, Marc Clegg, Katie Goad and all other dorm buddies, Mum and Dad, Alice, Tom and Annie, Granmum and Grandad, Griddy, Lesley Raphael, Jools Voce, Ed Havard, Mags and Oriane, Emma Freud, Emma Kennedy, Perks, Hadders, Amelia Watts, Baz Hilton, Emily, Cheryl and Heidi, Emma Strain, Zazie, Zoz and Jamie Polk.

Do you wish this wasn't the end?

Join us at www.hodder.co.uk, or follow us on
Twitter @hodderbooks to be a part of our community
of people who love the very best in books and reading.

Whether you want to discover more about a book
or an author, watch trailers and interviews, have the
chance to win early limited editions, or simply browse
our expert readers' selection of the very best books,
we think you'll find what you're looking for.

And if you don't,
that's the place to tell us what's missing.

We love what we do, and we'd love you to be part of it.

www.hodder.co.uk

@hodderbooks

HodderBooks

HodderBooks